# THE RAVAGES OF
# REJECTION

# THE RAVAGES OF
# REJECTION

## REJECTION WILL RAVAGE YOU
## OR REFINE YOU

(Praise is a Means of Taking Back Territory from the devil!)

## BISHOP JOEY JOHNSON

XULON PRESS

Xulon Press
2301 Lucien Way #415
Maitland, FL 32751
407.339.4217
www.xulonpress.com

Printed in the United States of America.

ISBN: 9781545608739

To Jason King who suggested that this material
be put in book form.


To Pat Butler who supports me administratively.


To Pat Reese who helps proof read my material.


To my wife, Cathy Johnson, who supports me
with love.


To the Father, the Son, and the Holy Spirit who
support me with love and life.

# Table of Contents

# Foreword

Rejection is one of the most common, harrowing, and traumatizing of human experiences. Yet, rejection probably originated with Lucifer himself. He personally rebelled against God and fomented a rebellion among the angels of heaven against God. In the act of rebellion is the seed of rejection. "Rejection" is a very broad concept and very difficult to define. But, a simple definition is "to refuse to accept or acknowledge" (*WordWeb Pro 8.04a*).

The devil refused to accept or acknowledge the reign and authority of God. God is a God of love and acceptance, but the devil is a being of hatred and rejection.

In fact, acceptance is integral to the Old Testament priestly ritual. "Priestly ritual is therefore the means by which Yahweh can 'accept' (root **rsh**) Israel. This concept of acceptance is central to the 'gospel' of Priestly Writing. The competence needed to offer sacrifices that can find acceptance by Yahweh was pivotal to the priest's profession (Lev. 19:5, 7; 22:19-29; compare the old 'job description' of Deut. 33:11). Naturally, the purpose of offering such acceptable sacrifices was that the worshippers themselves might be accepted (Lev. 1:3-4; 7:18). Thus, the priest raised the sheaf of the first fruits, so, the nation might find acceptance by God (Lev. 23:11). The plate on the high priest's turban had the same purpose (Exod. 28:38)."[1]

In the New Testament, we find these words:

> Ephesians 1:3-6 (KJV), "[3] Blessed *be* the God and Father of our Lord Jesus Christ, who hath blessed us with all spiritual blessings in heavenly *places* in Christ: [4] According as he hath chosen us in him before the foundation of the world, that we should be holy and without blame before him in love: [5]

---

[1] Richard D. Nelson, *Raising Up a Faithful Priest: Community and Priesthood in Biblical Theology*, Westminster/John Knox Press, Louisville, Kentucky, 1993, p. 129.

Having predestinated us unto the adoption of children by Jesus Christ to himself, according to the good pleasure of his will, [6] To the praise of the glory of his grace, wherein he hath made us accepted in the beloved."

As Christians, we are accepted in the Beloved, i.e. Jesus!

Whereas, the devil comes to kill, steal, and destroy! Are these not the outgrowths of rejection?

Furthermore, human sin is a rejection of God, His love, His provisions, and His wishes. Adam and Eve rejected God's restrictions and chose instead to listen to the serpent in the Garden of Eden. Inherent in accepting the words of the serpent is the rejection of God's words.

In this book, we'll work through a sermon series that I preached on the satanic nature of rejection and its impact upon the Children of Israel. In so doing, we'll see how praise is a means of overcoming satanic rejection. "Rejection will either ravage you or refine you!" I pray that this material will aid you in being refined, rather than ravaged.

Bishop Joey Johnson

# Chapter I

# The Satanic Nature of Rejection

On Monday morning, March 8th, 1999, God began to speak to me about a passage of Scripture in my daily Bible reading. The passage was

Deuteronomy 1:26-33 (NASB), "²⁶ Yet you were not willing to go up, but rebelled against the command of the LORD your God; ²⁷ and you grumbled in your tents and said, 'Because the LORD hates us, He has brought us out of the land of Egypt to deliver us into the hand of the Amorites to destroy us. ²⁸ Where can we go up? Our brethren have made our hearts melt, saying, "The people are bigger and taller than we; the cities are large and fortified to heaven. And besides, we saw the sons of the Anakim there."' [29] Then I said to you, 'Do not be shocked, nor fear them. [30] The LORD your God who goes before you will Himself fight on your behalf, just as He did for you in Egypt before your eyes, [31] and in the wilderness where you saw how the LORD your God carried you, just as a man carries his son, in all the way which you have walked until you came to this place.' [32] But for all this, you did not trust the LORD your God, [33] who goes before you on *your* way, to seek out a place for you to encamp, in fire by night and cloud by day, to show you the way in which you should go."

After reading these verses, I went to my computer and began to list the ravages or destructive effects of rejection that I saw. Because of some earlier sermon series, I had concluded that rejection is one of the most formidable psychological, emotional foes of Mankind. Rejection is keeping most people from experiencing the wonderful relationship that God has ordained Christianity to be. Belief in Jesus Christ is intended to bring about deep connectivity to Jehovah God, Jesus Christ, the Holy Spirit, other believers, and one's self, but the ravages of rejection block connectivity. I see it all the time in biblically counseling the members of our church.

Yet, I didn't want to continue to talk about rejection—despite the importance of the subject—then God began to reveal to me that rejection is more than a psychological, emotional, and interpersonal problem. **Rejection is a satanic stronghold!**

**A satanic stronghold is an area or place in a group or person's life where Satan has gained territory, because of sin, self, sickness, or the world.** In the passage of Scripture before us, the Children of Israel had allowed Satan to gain territory in their lives, because of the impact of the sin of slavery. The impact of the sin that was perpetrated against them opened a place, gate, or opportunity for Satan to work in their lives.

Egypt had enslaved the nation of Israel and foisted upon them cruel bondage. That cruel bondage had deeply impacted the Israelites in a very negative way. **They felt deeply rejected, as we shall see in the passage. I don't think that is hard to see, but what is hard to see is that this rejection and its ravages are satanic.** The power of this rejection flows from the spirit of evil, i.e. the devil and all his demons.

The rejection that the Israelites experienced, because of Egyptian slavery, was satanic. **The wickedness of the Egyptians went beyond not believing in Jehovah God; they served all kinds of false gods.** Paul explains in the New Testament that there are no such things as idol gods, but behind every idol god there is a demon. So, the powers of Egypt lie in the demonic. It is interesting that when God got ready to deliver the children of Israel from the cruel bondage of Egypt, He mentioned their gods. **He said that He was going to execute judgment against all the gods of Egypt (Exodus 12:12).**

Furthermore, Moses sang of the Israelites' bondage to demons in

Deuteronomy 32:17 (NASB), "¹⁷ **They sacrificed to demons who were not God**, To gods whom they have not known, New *gods* who came lately, Whom your fathers did not dread" (*bold type added*).

So, these demonic powers had a very debilitating effect upon the Israelites. **The satanic stronghold of rejection had entrapped the Israelites. Long after the children of Israel were out of Egypt, Egypt was still in the Children of Israel.** Let's touch on a little background of these verses. The name "Deuteronomy" means the second giving of the Law. The Children of Israel are now camped in front of the Promised Land. They had been wandering through the wilderness for 40 years, while everyone 20 years old and older who had **not** trusted God to take them into the Promised Land the first time died as chastisement from God. Moses is now looking back over the past 40 years, as he talks to them about finally entering the Promised Land. Moses is looking in the rear-view mirror of history. As I was riding in my car on Friday, March 12, 1999, I saw these words stenciled in white on the outside rearview mirror: **"Objects In Mirror Are Closer Than They Appear**." Israel's past was closer than it appeared. Forty (40) years appeared to be the distant past, but it was closer than it appeared. The past was still effecting their present. Even though rejection had blocked their trust in God forty (40) years ago, Moses knew that rejection was still impacting Israel in the present. Isn't it the same with us today? Hasn't the impact of *slavery (physical, psychological, emotional*, etc.) created a stronghold of rejection that is still impacting us in the present? So, to begin to understand the satanic stronghold of rejection, let's start to talk about the ravages of rejection.

**Understand that Satan is a master craftsman who crafts, in hell, devices of rejection for our destruction.** Look at the device of rejection that he crafted for the Israelites. Satan's main objective, at this point, was to stop the Children of Israel from obtaining the Promised Land. He did **not** want them to gain their inheritance or destiny. So, he used rejection to stop them. Here are the ravages or destructive effects that I see in this passage of Scripture:

- Unwillingness to obey God;
- Rebellion;
- Grumbling;
- Incorrect perception of God;
- Incorrect perception of God's destiny for them;
- Susceptibility to negative emotions (fear);
- Susceptibility to negative reports;
- Improper perception of themselves;
- Blindness to God's prophecy;
- Blindness to God's past blessings;
- An Inability to trust God;
- Blindness to God's providence.

I see 12 destructive effects of rejection in this short passage of Scripture. Twelve is the number of governmental perfection. **Satan is trying to perfect his evil government over the lives of the Children of Israel through rejection.**

Now some of you probably want to know "Where do you see rejection in the text?" That's an excellent question! You don't see rejection directly in the text. What you see is the negative impact of rejection. **But, one of the most telltale signs of rejection is the inability to perceive God correctly and the negativity of that perception.**

7

## Ravage #1: The Satanic Stronghold of Rejection

How did the Children of Israel perceive God? They give their perception in

> Deuteronomy 1:26, "...the LORD hates us..."

Therefore, they perceived God as personally hating them!

*This is shocking to me, because this is the exact antithesis or opposite of the nature and character of God!* John states specifically in

> 1 John 4:8 (NASB-U), "The one who does not love does not know God, for **God is love**" (*bold type added*).

Secondarily, how could they believe that God hated them, after all that He had done for them? He had:

- Delivered them from the bondage of Egypt;
- Led them by a pillar of cloud by day and a pillar of fire by night;

8

- Caused water to follow them underground;
- Sent manna from heaven;
- Caused their shoes to last for forty years;
- Not allowed their feet to swell for forty years;
- Protected them from fierce enemies;
- Etc., etc., etc.

The only thing that God hadn't done for them was take them into the Promised Land and that was because of their own disbelief, disobedience, and rebellion. *How could that one unfulfilled promise, which He was about to fulfill, stack up against all the other fulfilled promises of God? Answer: the impact of rejection deceived them.* Rejection caused them to focus on the negatives of their past and the negatives of their present situation, which distorted their perception of God. This is **not** just natural—this is supernatural. *A stronghold of rejection is at operation. This created a rejection paradigm.*

*This has pertinent, immediate, powerful application to where we are as a nation, a church, and individually.* Please note that the ancient Israelite culture is collectivistic, not individualistic. Consequently, it is group-oriented and the pertinent verses were written to the nation of Israel—not to individual Israelites. They exist for the group, while, in our culture, the group exists for the individual. These are two very different cultural maps. Cultural maps allow those in the culture to get things in their proper places.

Yet, even though these verses were not written to individuals, if we are respectful of the collectivistic culture, we can apply the revealed truths to us, as individuals.

With that caveat, let's begin with a major truth.

> Our perception of God will largely define and determine the relationship and fellowship that we are going to have with Him and that concept is built upon our conception of God.

Conception is concerned with how one thinks about or understands something. Perception has more to do with understanding something through the senses. We'll be working with the dynamic and powerful relationship of conception and perception.

If Satan can distort our perception, this will have a negative effect on our relationship and fellowship with God, and one of Satan's tools to this end is rejection.

*I talk to, advise, disciple, and help many people, and very often I see a stronghold of rejection their lives.* If we are honest with ourselves and we are in touch with what we feel, most of us feel that God does **not** care for us. Despite all the reading of the Word of God, all the sermons, and all the blessings of God, deep within we still feel that God doesn't like us. This is a milder way of saying that God hates us. We think as the Israelites think.

What did the Israelites think? "If God loves me:
- Why did He allow us to be enslaved?
- Why did He allow slavery to impact us so negatively?
- Why hasn't He given us the Promised Land?
- Why do we have to fight to obtain the Promised Land?
- Why do our enemies look so large?

- Why do we look so small in our own eyes?"

These thoughts and questions plague us and rob us of our inheritance and our destiny, but they are more than thoughts—they are satanic strongholds connected to rejection. Rejection distorted their perception of their circumstances, and what they saw had a great deal of effect on what they thought about God.

***Now this is where the deception starts!*** You are probably thinking, "But I haven't been deeply rejected!" Oh, haven't you?

- If you are African-American the residue of slavery has affected you—whether you are aware of it or not.
- If you are of another minority ethnic group, the residue of prejudice has affected you— whether you are aware of it or not.
- No matter what your ethnicity, we have all been affected by the rejection of Family Mess in our families.

American families have been struggling for a long time, and even good ones cannot be perfect.

- If you are a woman, you have received rejection that is connected to your gender.
- If you are physically challenged, you have likely experienced outright rejection.
- Etc., etc., etc.

***Therefore, we have all been affected by rejection at some level!***

***Furthermore, rejection is one of the major impacts of sin.***

- Satan rejected God. Then,
- Satan infected Adam and Eve and they rejected God. Then,
- Adam and Eve rejected each other.

When they rejected God, they separated or disconnected themselves from intimate fellowship with God. This brought about deep feelings of rejection within them. Even though God responded to them graciously and did **not** reject them, they still sensed and felt rejection because of the stronghold of rejection that was set up in them through their own rebellion and perception.

I don't think people understand this yet, "We feel love when we can positively ***respond*** to love;

13

we feel rejection when we ***project*** rejection!" Did you get that? It is **not** people loving you that make you feel loved; it is your response to their love. It is **not** people rejecting you that make you feel rejection; it is the reflection of your projection of rejection that gives you feelings of rejection. The rejection that Eve projected onto God caused her to think, "God has rejected me and God cannot be a good God, because He won't let me eat from the tree of the knowledge of good evil." Now, God had given them all the other trees of the Garden, but they were deceived about this one tree.

The point is: "Most of us have been rejected and are experiencing the effect of that rejection somewhere in our lives—even when we don't realize it or are unwilling to recognize it!" *The Truism is "Hurt people hurt people!" It is also true that people who feel rejected reject themselves, others, and ultimately God. They generally try to reject others, before others can reject them!*

However, I want to move this discussion to an even deeper level. I want to talk about the stronghold of rejection in a very specific way. Edgardo

Silvoso of Harvest Evangelism gives this definition of a stronghold:

> "a stronghold is a mindset impregnated with hopelessness that causes the believer to accept as unchangeable something that he/she knows is contrary to the will of God."[1]
>
> ---
> [1] Edgardo Silvoso, taken from a memorandum to supporters and friends on "Plan Resistencia," September 15, 1990: p. 3.

*(Let's apply this definition to the Israelites.)*

- Did the Israelites have a mindset impregnated with hopelessness?

Yes, they were hopeless about occupying the Promised Land, even though God had delivered them from Egypt with His mighty arm and preserved them for forty years.

- Did this mindset of hopelessness cause the Israelites to accept as unchangeable something that they knew was contrary to the will of God?

Yes! They were aware of the will of God, which was to give them the Promised Land. Nevertheless, the Children of Israel accepted their status in the wilderness as unchangeable. This was not merely natural, but supernatural. *The spirit of evil was working in the situation.*

Is God starting to reveal anything to you yet? *(Let's apply the definition to ourselves.)*

Are there areas in our lives where we have a mindset of hopelessness that causes us to accept as unchangeable something that we know is contrary to the will of God? Let me suggest some areas that I see in our lives:

## Abundant Christian Life

- Are we hopeless about ever experiencing the abundant Christian life or victory?
- Do we know that God wants us to be victorious and experience abundant Christian life and yet we are stuck in a mindset of hopelessness—**not** knowing how to break free from this mindset?

- Do we see this mindset as unchangeable?
- Are we blaming God with words like, "I've done all that I can, so why won't God do something about my situation?"

If we answered "Yes!" to several these questions, there may be a **satanic** stronghold our lives.

## Marriage

- Are we hopeless about enjoying a marriage that will glorify God?
- Are we aware of the biblical fact that God wants us to have a God-glorifying marriage, but we seem trapped in a mindset of hopelessness about our marriage?
- Has that hopelessness degenerated into bitterness and now numbness? Are we now numb to teaching on marriage, numb about having a better marriage, numb about wanting to have a better marriage, believing it is impossible to have a better marriage?
- Are we skipping Marriage Retreats because of hopelessness? Is our mindset unchangeable?

17

If we answered "Yes!" to several these questions, there may be a ***satanic*** stronghold in our lives.

## Singleness

- Are you hopeless about enjoying singleness and glorifying God?
- Are you aware of God's plan for singles, but yet hopeless that you will ever achieve or experience God's plan and ideal for your life?
- Have you accepted the loneliness of your singleness as unchangeable?

If you answered "Yes!" to several these questions, there may be a ***satanic*** stronghold in our lives.

## Relationships

- Are we hopeless about having genuine, godly, edifying relationships?
- Are we aware of the elevated level of relationships that God wants for us, but still hopeless that we can ever experience those kinds of relationships.

- Have we given up on relationships, because we have lost a few relationships and are protecting ourselves?
- Have we accepted as unchangeable the shallow, negative, stressed relationships that we have, even though we know that they are contrary to God's will for our lives?

If we answered "Yes!" to several these questions, there may be a **satanic** stronghold in our lives.

## Church

- Are we hopeless about the Church of Jesus Christ?
- Are we hopeless about what God is doing in His Church?
- Are we hopeless that the Church of Jesus Christ can be what God wants it to be?
- Do we know the will of God for His Church in this age, but still accept as unchangeable those things that we see as contrary to the will of God?

- Do we refuse to identify our spiritual gifts, find a ministry and get involved, because of our negative view of the church?

If we answered "Yes!" to several these questions, there may be a ***satanic*** stronghold in our lives.

Now, since we are dealing with the ***satanic*** stronghold of rejection, the ultimate solution is **not** a ***psychological*** one, but a ***spiritual*** one. The question is "How do we defeat the power of ***satanic*** strongholds in our lives? ***How do we take back territory that has been lost to the Devil?***"

Keep in mind that "On the Divine side, the victory has been won, and Satan and his deceiving spirits have been conquered, but the actual liberation of the believer demands his ACTIVE CO-OPERATION WITH THE HOLY SPIRIT, and the steady exercise of his volition, choosing freedom instead of bondage, and the normal use of every faculty of his being, set at liberty from the bondage of the enemy."[2]

---

[2] Jessie Penn-Lewis, War On The Saints, The Christian Literature Crusade, Fort Washington, Pennsylvania, 1977, p. 102.

All right, are you tired of wandering in the wilderness; the wilderness of Christianity; the wilderness of marriage, the wilderness of singleness; the wilderness of parenting; the wilderness of sickness; the financial wilderness? Well, one of the ways that we take back land that God has promised to us is to resist the devil.

> James 4:7 (NASB-U), "Submit therefore to God. Resist the devil and he will flee from you."

*(Once again, the question comes up, "How do we resist the devil?" There are at least seven ways that we can resist the devil, but we are only going to work on one of them: praise.)*

***Praise is a means of taking back territory from the devil!***

I will explain this more in the coming chapters. But, remember: praise can position rejection to be more refining, than ravaging!

## Chapter 2

# Rejection Blocks Obedience to God

Drop a coin on a sidewalk and almost every eye will follow it, but drop a needy child in a community and very few will pay attention. Case in point—little Joseph who had polio. Someone finally took him to Sunday school, but the teacher neglected him. Later the young people subjected him to ridicule and avoided him because of his crippled condition. As a result, he dropped out of the class with a hatred for the church and the Lord Jesus Christ. However, he continued his studies in school. When he finally earned his doctorate from Heidelberg University, a man slipped his arm around him, saying, "Joseph, I think a lot of you; you and I could do much together."

The young fellow responded warmly to this welcomed attention and encouragement, and in time Joseph Goebbels became the propaganda minister for that man: Adolf Hitler!

As we work our way through Deuteronomy 1:26-33, remember that we don't see the word "rejection," but we do see the **negative impact** and the **destructive results** of rejection. The Children of Israel were horribly rejected through the **satanic device of slavery**, down in Egypt, but their slavery entailed more than natural bondage. **Their slavery entailed a spiritual bondage that was wrapped up with the idol gods and demons of the Egyptian religion. Even though God had gotten the Children of Israel out of slavery, He was still working to get slavery out of the Children of Israel.** The past is often like the stenciled letters on my rearview mirror: "**OBJECTS IN MIRROR ARE CLOSER THAN THEY APPEAR**." *Often, what we consider to be the past is still very much a part of the present!*

*The first listed effect of rejection is disobedience.* God indicts the Israelites as **not** being willing to go up and take the Promised Land as He had commanded, i.e. the first time they were camped in front of the Promised Land. The word "willing" in the NASB is also translated "obey" in another place in the Bible. The KJV states, "... you would not go up." ***The Israelites refused to obey God.***

Now, what caused this blatant disobedience? ***Well, there are a probably several causes, but certainly one of the main ones is an incorrect perception of God.*** In the last chapter, we touched on their perception that God hated them. Consequently, how could they trust a God who they believed hated them? They couldn't! Moreover, they couldn't obey a God that they couldn't trust, because of how they viewed Him!

At this point, we are beginning to discuss another destructive effect of rejection, disbelief or a lack of trust in God. It is so intertwined with the story that we must begin to discuss it now, even though we will explore this phenomenon later.

Now, the writer of the sermon to the Hebrews says that the Children of Israel are an example to Christians. This is often, as in this case, a negative example. ***In fact, in the 3rd and 4th chapters of the sermon to the Hebrews, the writer correlates the Israelites' failure to enter the***

*Promised Land with our inability to enter God's rest, i.e. the present Promised Land of abundant Christian living.* The Promised Land for us is a life that is lived by resting in the Lord. The Bible reads in

> Hebrews 4:2, "For indeed we have had good news preached to us, just as they also; but the word they heard did not profit them, because it was not united by faith in those who heard."

The good news of the Promised Land was preached to the Israelites, but it did **not** profit them because they did **not** believe in or trust Jehovah God.

*Likewise, the good news of the Gospel of Jesus and the supernatural rest of victorious Christian living, which is our Promised Land, have been preached to us and we are in danger of it <u>not</u> profiting us because of a lack of faith or trust in Jehovah God.*

Are you getting the sequence that I am trying to illustrate?

Rejection may ⇨ a satanic stronghold of rejection ⇨ an incorrect perception of God ⇨ a lack of trust in God ⇨ disobedience.

The disobedience in Deuteronomy was to the will of God. God wanted them to go up and take the Promised Land, but they were unwilling to do so.

Remember that we are treating rejection as a satanic stronghold. Edgardo Silvoso of Harvest Evangelism gives this definition of a stronghold:

"a stronghold is a mindset impregnated with hopelessness that causes the believer to accept as unchangeable something that he/she knows is contrary to the will of God."[1]

[1] Edgardo Silvoso, taken from a memorandum to supporters and friends on "Plan Resistencia," September 15, 1990: p. 3.

Are we blatantly disobeying God because of the satanic stronghold of rejection? Consider the following areas:

- **Giving**.

*Are we selfishly disobedient to God in our giving?*
We know that we should be giving to God, but we
are unwilling to do so and continue to act selfishly
and disobediently.

  ➢ Why? Because we don't trust God to take
    care of us.
  ➢ Why? Because of our misperception of God.
  ➢ Why? Because of a stronghold of rejection.

Our mindsets about God's providential care
have been impregnated with hopelessness and that
hopelessness causes us to accept as unchangeable our financial plight and our view of God's
character—even though we know that this view
is contrary to the will of God.

- Victory.

*We know that God wants us to live victorious
Christian lives, but we are unwilling and continue
to disobey God and think defeated thoughts.*

  ➢ Why? Because we don't trust God to give us
    spiritual victory.
  ➢ Why? Because of our misperception of God.
  ➢ Why? Because of a stronghold of rejection.

We have been so rejected that Satan has impregnated our minds with hopelessness concerning victory, which causes us to accept as unchangeable our defeat at the hands of the enemy—even though we know that this is contrary to the will of God.

*We can apply this understanding to any area of our lives, but keep in mind that there is more here than a psychological or emotional impact of rejection.* That is why rejection **sometimes** does **not** respond to counseling and may **not** be healed through counseling alone. *The root of rejection is a satanic stronghold, and we are trying to treat a <u>spiritual</u> root with a <u>psychological</u> root killer.*

In this book, I'm working on only one spiritual antidote to the stronghold of rejection: praise. Praise is a means of taking back territory from the devil! The Children of Israel should have occupied the Promised Land in God's timing, but they refused to obey God. Now, in a sense, they would need to take back territory that was lost because of disobedience.

Praise and worship are more than elements of church worship services, praise and worship are

tools that are designed to usher in the final manifestation of God's kingdom.

I define "praise" as the verbal acclaiming of God,
because of what He has done for you. I define "worship" as giving God whatever He is due, because
of who He is!

Amos prophesies of a praise and worship
movement in

> Amos 9:11-12 (NIV), "'In that day I
> will restore David's fallen tent. I will
> repair its broken places, restore its
> ruins, and build it as it used to be, so
> that they may possess the remnant of
> Edom and all the nations that bear my
> name,' declares the LORD, who will do
> these things."

Scholars are divided over the meaning of the
phrase "David's fallen tent." It seems certain that
Amos is talking about the house of David, i.e.
the Messianic line. However, other scholars see
Amos as prophesying about the praise and worship that were so characteristic of David's reign.

While still other scholars see Amos as including both meanings.

I get excited every time I read these verses, because God is fulfilling an awesome prophecy in our times. ***"David's fallen tent refers to what has become known as the tabernacle of David."***[3] David took the Ark of the Covenant from the Tabernacle of Moses, which was still set up at Gibeon, and placed it in a special tent on Mount Zion. In addition, David consecrated singers, musicians, and prophets to continually minister before the Ark. Remember, only the High Priest, once a year, with blood for himself and the people, could enter the Holy of holies of the Tabernacle of Moses; and even then, he entered with fear and trembling. But, musicians, singers, and prophets ministered continually before the Ark of the Covenant, in David's tabernacle, based on David's relationship with Jehovah God! The first tabernacle was a place of **rules** and **ritual**, but David's tabernacle, where the Ark of the Covenant was set up, was a place of **relationship** and **rejoicing**. "In the Old Testament, it

---

[3] Robert Gay, *Silencing The Enemy*, Creation House, Orlando, Florida, 1993, pp. 12-13.

(*The Tabernacle of David*) was the ultimate place of worship—a place of continual praise."[4]

**The exciting thing is that God is restoring this fallen tent of David.** God is restoring the wondrous relationship and rejoicing that David experienced during his stay on earth. That restoration began on the Great Day of Pentecost and it is still growing. On the Great Day of Pentecost, the gift of the Holy Spirit was poured out; the Holy Spirit came to the earth in a completely new way and made possible a completely new kind of **relationship with** and **praise of** Jehovah God, paid for by Jesus Christ, through the power of the Holy Spirit. **God now lives inside of us and our praise is set on fire by the Holy Spirit Himself.**

The fact that the restoration of the tabernacle of David began on the Great Day of Pentecost is proven by the words of James. In the first council of the Church, at Jerusalem, James correlated Amos' prophecy with what God was doing among the Gentiles (Acts 15:13-18). James said in

---

[4]   Robert Gay, *Silencing the Enemy*, Creation House, Orlando, Florida, 1993, pp. 12-13.

Acts 15:15-16 (NASB-U), "With this the words of the Prophets agree, just as it is written, [16] 'AFTER THESE THINGS I WILL RETURN, AND I WILL REBUILD THE TABERNACLE OF DAVID WHICH HAS FALLEN, AND I WILL REBUILD ITS RUINS, AND I WILL RESTORE IT.'"

James applied Amos' prophecy to what God was doing among the Gentiles, which was the fulfilling of

Acts 1:8 (NASB-U), "But you will receive power when the Holy Spirit has come upon you; and you shall be My witnesses both in Jerusalem, and in all Judea and Samaria, and even to the remotest part of the earth."

This prophecy was fulfilled in Jerusalem in Acts 2:4; in Judea in Acts 8; and in Samaria in Acts 10. So, the baptism in the Holy Spirit, which was spreading out according to Acts 1:8 is the rebuilding of the praise and worship that was characteristic of the Tabernacle of David, which had fallen. God was rebuilding the ruins of that praise and worship and restoring it!

*Amos also gives God's reasoning for restoring the fallen tent of David: to possess the remnant of Edom. Edom was related to Israel, but an enemy.* The word "'possess' is the Hebrew word **yaresh**, which means to 'occupy by driving out the previous tenants, to cast out, to consume, to destroy, to disinherit.'"[5] *Could it be that the Church is experiencing a revival of praise and worship, because they are to be used as instruments of warfare in possessing what is rightfully ours by promise? I believe the answer is "Yes!"*

Let's apply this to ourselves. Satan and his evil horde have been able to take territory in our spirits by impregnating our minds with hopelessness concerning the things that God has already promised to us. *Those things that are in our minds, hearts, and spirits come out of us through our mouths.* I don't believe in name and claim it, stab it and grab it, call it and haul it, but

---

[5] Robert Gay, *Silencing the Enemy*, Creation House, Orlando, Florida, 1993, p. 14.

I do believe that the Bible teaches a principle of the importance of our words. The Bible says in

> Matthew 12:37, "For by your words you shall be justified, and by your words you shall be condemned."

Understanding this, we must begin to change our speech. Certainly, we must change our hearts, but if we are having trouble changing our hearts we can start with our words.

The writer of the Proverbs wrote in

> Proverbs 18:21, "Death and life are in the power of the tongue, and those who love it will eat its fruit."

*It is very interesting to me that the Children of Israel got what they spoke.* They said, "You hate us and have brought us out here to die." That was a lie, but it was a self-fulfilling prophecy. It reminds me of the steward who said, "I know you to be harsh man who reaps where he has not sown." Consequently, the master said, in effect, "I will judge you according to those words!

We are speaking negative, self-fulfilling prophecies through the negative words that we speak. These negative words flow out of our perception of God, which is impacted by the stronghold of rejection.

*(So, what are we to do?)*

In short,

- We must stop speaking words of hopelessness and start speaking words of hope.
- We must stop speaking our rejection-based perceptions of God and start speaking God's revealed words concerning Himself.
- We must stop speaking the devil's damnation and start speaking God's destiny.

When we praise the name of Jesus, we are proclaiming the exact opposite of what Satan wants us to proclaim.

- Satan says, "Don't you know that God hates you?" However, we say, "Our God is a loving God who loves us with an everlasting love!"
- Satan says, "Don't you know that God doesn't care about you?" We say, "Our God is a compassionate God, who loves us with an everlasting love!"

- Satan says, "Don't you know that God doesn't care about what happens to you?" We proclaim, "Our God is a God of destiny, and He has a destiny for us.

*When we praise God, we take back territory in our mouths, in our minds, in our hearts, and in our spirits, that had been controlled by the devil. This will open us up to obey God, because our perception of God is being changed and we are learning to trust Him.*

Therefore, our resolve ought to be:

Psalm 34:1, "I will bless the LORD at all times; His praise shall continually be in my mouth."

Chapter 3

# Rejection Effects Rebellion Against God's Commands

## Weak but Strong

The famous blind songwriter, Fanny Crosby, wrote more than 8,000 songs. When Fanny was only 6 weeks old a minor eye inflammation developed. The doctor who treated the case was careless, though, and she became totally and permanently blind. ***Fanny Crosby harbored no bitterness against the physician, however.*** In fact, she once said of him, "If I could meet him now, I would say thank you, thank you, over and over again for making me blind." ***She felt that her blindness was a gift from God to*** *help her write the hymns that flowed from her pen.* According to those who knew her, Miss Crosby probably would have refused treatment even if it could have assured the restoration of her sight. One biographer commented, "It was said of another blind hymnwriter, George Matheson, that God made him blind so he could see clearly in other ways and become a guide to men. This same tribute could be applied to Fanny Crosby, who triumphed over her handicap and used it to the glory of God." *Yes, this talented woman allowed her tragedy to make her <u>better</u> instead of <u>bitter</u>.*

Fanny Crosby did **not** let bitterness ruin her, because she saw herself as *blessed* by God instead of *cursed*. She evidently understood something about God's nature and considered her blindness as an act of God's acceptance of her, rather than His rejection. *Therefore, instead of grumbling against God, she thanked Him.*

We are working on the ravages of rejection that I see in

> Deuteronomy 1:26-33 (NASB), "²⁶ Yet you were not willing to go up, but rebelled against the command of the

LORD your God; [27] and you grumbled in your tents and said, 'Because the LORD hates us, He has brought us out of the land of Egypt to deliver us into the hand of the Amorites to destroy us. [28] Where can we go up? Our brethren have made our hearts melt, saying, "The people are bigger and taller than we; the cities are large and fortified to heaven. And besides, we saw the sons of the Anakim there." [29] Then I said to you, "Do not be shocked, nor fear them. [30] The LORD your God who goes before you will Himself fight on your behalf, just as He did for you in Egypt before your eyes, [31] and in the wilderness where you saw how the LORD your God carried you, just as a man carries his son, in all the way which you have walked until you came to this place." [32] But for all this, you did not trust the LORD your God, [33] who goes before you on *your* way, to seek out a place for you to encamp, in fire by night and cloud by day, to show you the way in which you should go.'"

*The next listed, destructive effect of rejection is rebellion. Rebellion is opposition to the one who is in authority.* Therefore, from a strict definitive perspective, what we see is rebellion towards God's authority. The text gives us the object of this rebellion, which is the specific command of Jehovah to go up and take the Promised Land.

*Please understand that the command of one who is in authority represents that one's authority.* However, a deeper look at the Hebrew word will give us additional information. The Hebrew word is **marah**. *Strong's Greek & Hebrew Dictionary* says that the word means "bitter." Have you heard the word **marah** before? If you are a Bible reader, you have.

After God drowned the Egyptians in the Red Sea, by His mighty outstretched arm, Miriam led the women of Israel in a dance of praise, and Moses then led the Children of Israel into the wilderness of Shur. On this journey, they traveled for three days without any water, but finally arrived at **Marah**. However, they couldn't drink the waters, because they were bitter. The Bible literally reads in

Exodus 15:23, "And when they came to the waters of **Marah**, they couldn't drink the waters of **Marah**, for they were **marah**; therefore it was called **Marah**" (*bold type added*).

Hebrew has a very small vocabulary; therefore, the word Marah, which means bitter, is used repeatedly. ***The Children of Israel were bitter against the command of the Lord.*** The word translated "command" is literally "mouth." The Israelites were bitter against the "mouth" or Word of God. If they were bitter against the "mouth" of God, weren't they bitter against God? The answer is "Yes!"

***Bitterness is anger turned sour, and anger is a strong feeling of displeasure or antagonism.*** Like milk that sours without refrigeration, so anger held in one's **hot** heart sours into bitterness. Paul tells us in:

Hebrews 12:15 (NASB), "See to it that no one comes short of the grace of God; that no root of bitterness springing up causes trouble, and by it many be defiled."

Bitterness affects the subject and those connected to him/her. Bitterness will trouble you and it will defile many others. ***Therefore, rebellion is one of the effects of the stronghold of rejection, and rebellion is the result of bitterness that flows from unresolved anger.***

***Now keep in mind that rebellion is demonic.*** A verse in 1 Samuel confirms this. It is interesting to note that the same Hebrew root word is used in

> 1 Samuel 15:23 (NASB), "For **rebellion** is as the sin of divination, and insubordination is as iniquity and idolatry. Because you have rejected the word of the LORD, he has also rejected you from being king" (*bold type added*).

The Hebrew word for "rebellion" comes from the same root as the word "marah." "Divination" is translated "witchcraft" in the KJV. The word means "the art or practice that seeks to foresee or foretell future events or discover hidden knowledge usually by the interpretation of omens or by the aid of supernatural powers."[6]

The Children of Israel were bitter, antagonistic, or rebellious against the directions of the LORD and opted to determine their own direction through the witchcraft of personal mysticism; and the stronghold of rejection was fueling their anger.

Aren't we experiencing the same thing? **Rejection makes us angry with God, when He gives us a command.** Hence, we try to determine our own direction through personal mysticism or the rationalism of one's own mind, or the wishing well, or tarot cards, or some other form of witchcraft.

We are talking about a stronghold!

---

[6]  *Merriam-Webster's Collegiate Dictionary, Tenth Edition with Merriam-Webster's Collegiate Thesaurus for Windows 95*, Version 3.1.1.401, ©1997, 1996 Zane Publishing, Inc.

"a stronghold is a mindset impregnated with hopelessness that causes the believer to accept as unchangeable something that he/she knows is contrary to the will of God."[1]

[1] Edgardo Silvoso, taken from a memorandum to supporters and friends on "Plan Resistencia," September 15, 1990; p. 3.

Alright, let's deal with one area of application: difficult circumstances!

The Children of Israel were angry with and rebelled against Moses, because they didn't have any water to drink. *Even though their anger and rebellion was directed at God's leader Moses, they were ultimately angry with God.* The rejection that they had experienced at the hands of the Egyptians had made them angry and bitter with God. There is no doubt that God had them on their present journey. They were only two weeks away from the Promised Land, when God took them another way, because He didn't want them to see war. God knew that they would change their minds about possessing the Promised Land, when they saw war. Therefore, God was ultimately responsible for their difficult circumstance of thirst. Perhaps God allowed them to thirst in the wilderness because He wanted them to thirst for Him; a thirst that He was going to fulfill in worship and in giving them the Promised Land.

*What difficult situations do we have in our lives where our mindset is impregnated with hopelessness and we have accepted bitterness as a way of life, even though we know that bitterness is contrary to the will of God?*

- Church.

    This area is most directly related to the situation of the Children of Israel. There are many people in our church and in every church, who are bitter with and rebel against the pastor and leadership, because of the direction of the church. Maybe these people don't realize that their bitterness and rebellion is ultimately against God. Why? Because

    - Either your pastor is the man or woman of God and leading the church according to the will of God, in which case God is directing the church.

- Or your pastor is the man or woman of God and not leading the church according to the will of God, in which case God is still in control and allowing the situation.
- Or your pastor is not the man or woman of God, but leading the church according to God's will despite himself, in which case God is directing the church in spite of that pastor.
- Or your pastor is not the man or woman of God and not leading the church according to the will of God, in which case God is still in control and allowing the situation.

*In all of these scenarios, God is still in ultimate control!*

Consequently, many of these people have accepted their bitterness against God's leader, and God Himself, as unchangeable—even though they know that this bitterness is contrary to the will of God and the commands of God.

- Marriage.

   *I see many spouses who are bitter and rebellious against their mates, because they view their marriages as difficult.* They may not understand that their bitterness is really against God, not *just* against their mates. God directed them or allowed them to marry the person to whom they are married. Therefore, they have accepted bitterness and rebellion as an unchangeable way of life, even though they know that bitterness is contrary to the commands of God, and God Himself.

- Singleness.

   *Many singles, <u>not</u> all of them, are bitter with life because of the loneliness that they face.* They may not know that their bitterness is really against God, who is sovereign and ultimately in control. They have accepted bitterness as an unchangeable way of life, even though they know that this bitterness is contrary to the will of God and to the commands of God. *Therefore, they rebel against God by having sex outside of God's prescribed, biblical commandments.*

- Relationships.

  I see many people who have experienced difficult situations with respect to their relationships. *They have become bitter about being rejected, let down, or abandoned any number of times.* They may not understand that their bitterness is really against God, whom they perceive as not blessing them for some unknown reason. They have accepted this bitterness with respect to their relationships as unchangeable, even though they know that this bitterness is contrary to the will of God and to the commands of God. Therefore, they rebel against God's word, will, and way with respect to pursuing loving, biblical relationships.

- Abundant Christian Life.

  I don't see many people bitter over their inability to experience the abundant Christian life. *They are _not_ bitter, because they have gone at least one step beyond bitterness.* I believe that hurt is one of the fundamental human feelings. I believe you can reduce all human feelings down to two: pain or pleasure. I believe one of the deepest levels of pain is hurt. Because we have a very difficult time facing hurt, we often cover our hurt with other feelings. *Anger is one of the emotions that many of us use to cover Hurt.* Anger is our processing emotion! Why? *Because, we are trying to protect our vulnerability that is exposed through hurt.*

Now there is a progression here.

- Hurt is covered by anger;
- Anger is covered by bitterness;
- Bitterness is covered by depression; and
- Depression is covered by revenge.

Therefore, we may not see many people angry about not obtaining an abundant Christian life. *Instead, they are depressed and listless with respect to abundant Christian life and victory.*

Consequently, many rebel against God's command towards abundant Christian living through their lethargy or hopelessness towards God's Word and God Himself.

By the way, the next verse, which is Deuteronomy 1:34, says that God heard the sound of their words and He got angry and took an oath that none of that evil generation would be allowed into the Promised Land except Caleb, because he was the only one who followed God fully. *It seems that their anger aroused God's anger. Therefore, it's not a good idea to be angry with God.*

Earlier, I mentioned the truth that praise is a means of taking back territory from the devil!

In addition, praise protects our personalities and spirits from further satanic attack.

The Bible uses the analogy or comparison of the walls of Jerusalem to the walls of a person's spirit/soul or personality. Jerusalem represents the immaterial part, i.e. the spirit/soul of the nation of Israel. The walls of the city represent the walls of human personality, and the gates of the city represent access and egress points of human personality. You can see this analogy in

Proverbs 25:28 (NASB-U), "Like a city that is broken into and without walls Is a man who has no control over his spirit."

*God has constructed our personalities with certain walls or boundaries for keeping out invaders and protecting us. Furthermore, God has constructed our personalities with gates, like the gates of a city.* Gates keep out what needs to be kept out, keep in what needs to be kept in, let out what needs to be let out, and let in what needs to be let in.

Therefore, we must rule our spirits and control the access and egress points of our personalities.

*When Satan's hellish device of rejection has done its destructive work, it tears down the walls of our personalities and burns the gates with fire.* Therefore, demons can come within the borders or boundaries of our personalities and occupy and control territory that they were never intended to control.

At salvation, the Holy Spirit takes up residence in the Holy of holies of our personalities and evicts anything and anyone evil—but we still need to rebuild the walls and re-hang the gates of our personalities. Therefore, because of broken-down walls and burned gates, demons return and seek to reassert their dominance. *If we do not cooperate with God in the rebuilding of the walls of our personalities and the re-hanging of our gates, Satan will regain lost territory.*

One remedy for the broken-down walls and gates of our personality is praise! *Praise protects our personalities and spirits from further satanic attack!* This is written in

> Isaiah 60:18 (NASB), "Violence will not be heard again in your land, Nor devastation or destruction within your borders; **But you will call your walls salvation, and your gates praise**" (*bold type added*).

### *"You will call your walls salvation, and your gates praise!"*

God is saying that He will appoint salvation as walls and defensive fortifications around the city of Jerusalem. God's deliverance will be their protection; God's aid will be their walls; God's victory, prosperity, deliverance, health, and help will be their walls and defensive fortifications.

Likewise, salvation, and all that it stands for in Jesus Christ, when it is fully experienced is the walls and defensive fortifications for our souls, spirits, or personalities.

*Note the point that the gates of Jerusalem shall be called "Praise."* Typologically, the gates of our personalities are praise. Now, what does that mean? I think it means that praise is one of the gates of our personalities. ***Praise ought to mark what we voluntarily let into our personalities, and praise ought to be what we voluntarily let out of our personalities.*** Therefore, praise is the sentinel or gatekeeper of our personalities!

- Praise will stand guard at the gates of our personality and keep out the evil one!
- Praise will stand guard at the access points into our personality and guard our hearts and minds with perfect peace.

Doesn't this sound like what Isaiah said in

Isaiah 26:3 (KJV), "Thou wilt keep him in perfect peace, whose mind is stayed on thee: because he trusteth in thee."

- Doesn't praise keep our minds stayed on God?
- Don't we praise God because our minds are stayed on Him?
- Then, won't He keep those who praise Him in perfect peace?

Finally,

- Praise will let out or evict everything that needs to be evicted from our spirits/souls or personalities. Praise will evict demons and evil from our innermost beings!

You can't habitually and genuinely praise God and be dominated by demons and evil!

Therefore, our resolve ought to be:

> Psalm 34:1 (NASB-U), "...I will bless the Lᴏʀᴅ at all times; His praise shall continually be in my mouth."

Cha

# Rejection Effects G

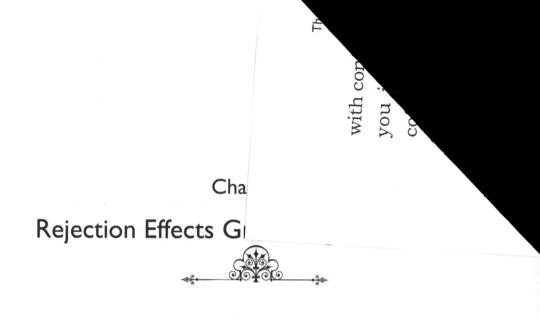

## Which Did God Believe?

A father asked the blessing at breakfast in his usual manner, thanking
God for what He had provided. After
he said "Amen," he resumed his habit
of grumbling about hard times, about
the poor quality of the food, about
the way it was cooked, and much
more. His little daughter listened with
unusual attention and dared to inter-
rupt him by saying, "Daddy, do you
think God heard what you said when
you prayed?" "Certainly," he responded

fidence. "And did He hear what just said about the bacon and fee?" "Of course," he replied meekly. "Then, Daddy, which did God believe?"

**W**hich do you think God believes? Your prayers or your pouting, your gratefulness or your grumbling!

I want to remind you that we are working through the ravaging effects of rejection in Deuteronomy 1:26-33. In this passage of Scripture, we don't really see the rejection of slavery. What we see is the **negative impact** and the **destructive results** of that rejection. The Children of Israel were horribly rejected through the **satanic device of slavery**, down in Egypt, but their slavery entailed more than natural bondage. **Their slavery entailed a spiritual bondage that was wrapped up with the idol gods and demons of the Egyptian religion. Even though God had gotten the Children of Israel out of slavery, He was still working to get slavery out of the Children of Israel.** The past is often like the stenciled letters on my rearview mirror: "**OBJECTS IN MIRROR ARE CLOSER THAN THEY APPEAR**." **Often, what** *we consider to be the past is still very much a part of the present!*

*The next listed, destructive effect of the stronghold of rejection is grumbling.* The text states that the Children of Israel grumbled in their tents. The Hebrew word is

> grumbled **ragan** *raw-gan'* [920d]; a primitive root; *to murmur, whisper* :- criticize(1), grumbled(2), slanderer(1), whisperer(3).[7]

The dictionary defines the word "grumble"

"**1** : to mutter in discontent."[8]

The dictionary defines the word "murmur" as

---

[7] NASB Dictionary.
[8] *Merriam-Webster's Collegiate Dictionary, Tenth Edition* with *Merriam-Webster's Collegiate Thesaurus* for Windows 95, Version 3.1.1.401, ©1997, 1996 Zane Publishing, Inc. All rights reserved.

"**1 :** a half-suppressed or muttered complaint."[9]

*The Israelites complained against God and their complaint was blaming God for their situation.* They didn't come out and blame God directly, they were too afraid to do that—but they grumbled in their tents.

*I have learned from years of discipling people and reading that anger is looking for someone to blame.* Anger does **not** take responsibility for anything that has happened. The Israelites believed that they had done everything right, while God was responsible for their demanding situation.

Now, what did they blame God for?

- They blamed God for hating them.
- They blamed God for bringing them out of Egypt to deliver them into the hands of their most fierce enemy, the Amorites.
- They blamed God for delivering them into the hands of the Amorites *to destroy them*.

---

[9] *Merriam-Webster's Collegiate Dictionary, Tenth Edition* with *Merriam-Webster's Collegiate Thesaurus* for Windows 95, Version 3.1.1.401, ©1997, 1996 Zane Publishing, Inc. All rights reserved.

*The Children of Israel were angry and bitter, because—in their perception—Jehovah God had not lived up to their expectations.*

- Even though He kept His word and delivered them from Egypt, after 400 years of bondage.
- Even though He protected them from war, by taking them on an alternate route to the Promised Land.
- Even though they refused to take the Promised Land, after the report of the twelve spies was given.

Yet, they blamed God for everything negative that had happened to them!

*Consequently, their misperception of God led to their grumbling and their grumbling further distorted their perception. This is a*

## "Negativity Feedback Loop!"

*Because of their perception of God, they grumbled against Him. At the same time, the more they grumbled against Him, the more their perception was ingrained, believed, and experienced.*

59

***Yet, God simply wanted them to trust and rely upon Him.*** According to Deuteronomy 29:2-6, all the divine providence of God was so that they might know that He was Jehovah and their God. However, they could **not** see this because of the Satanic stronghold of rejection, which distorted their perception.

***Let me remind you that Jehovah did eventually take the Children of Israel into the Promised Land, through Joshua, when the Walls of Jericho fell down with a shout!***

Throughout this book, we are treating the ravaging effects of rejection as a satanic stronghold.

Edgardo Silvoso of Harvest Evangelism gives this definition of a stronghold:

> "a stronghold is a mindset impregnated with hopelessness that causes the believer to accept as unchangeable something that he/she knows is contrary to the will of God."[1]
>
> ---
> [1]   Edgardo Silvoso, taken from a memorandum to supporters and friends on "Plan Resistencia," September 15, 1990: p. 3.

There are a series of questions that we want to entertain for application:

1. Where has God **not** lived up to your expectations?

2. Where has God **not** lived up to your expectations and you have prayed to Him about the situation, but there is **no** answer from heaven? In other words, where are the wilderness situations in your life?

3. Where have disappointed expectations and frustrated prayers caused you to become angry with God?

4. Where has your anger against God soured into bitterness?

5. Where has your bitterness become grumbling?

6. Where has that grumbling become a mindset impregnated with hopelessness?

7. Where has that mindset caused you to accept as unchangeable something that you know is contrary to the will of God?

I have taught, preached to, discipled, and prayed with thousands of believers, and some of the more prominent areas of disappointed expectations have to do with singleness, marriage, finance, health, and the loss of loved ones.

I'm convinced that most American's don't realize how rejected they are and the emotional impact of that rejection! ***Your depression, help-lessness, hopelessness, victimization, and even the symptoms of your illness are made worst because of rejection!***

As we consider this destructive effect of rejection, let's look at the area of happiness.

This area approximates the situation with the Children of Israel. "How so?" you ask. The Children of Israel had unrealistic expectations about their entrance into the Promised Land, and modern believers have unrealistic expectations concerning happiness.

***Happiness is connected to happenstance about some specific situation.*** By contrast, joy is supernatural and is experienced despite the circumstance. The Children of Israel apparently equated happiness with quick entry into the Promised Land, even though God hadn't given them a timetable.

Moreover, He hadn't promised that their entry, into the Promised Land, would be without difficulty or fighting. By contrast, modern believers equate happiness with trouble-free living or receiving things that they think they are entitled to. Even though God has never promised overall happiness to modern believers, they are often disappointed when they are not experiencing it. They are disappointed that God has not lived up to their specific expectations.

Not having received the happiness that they believe they are entitled to, many modern believers pray to God for some type of answer or explanation. Jehovah God *often* does **not** answer such prayers, because they are not concerned with having *an encounter* with Him or having *a relationship* with Him. James says in

> James 4:3, "You ask and do not receive, because you ask with wrong motives, so that you may spend it on your pleasures."

This is where the dry, wilderness experience begins to set in. We are disappointed in God, because He hasn't met our unbiblical/unrealistic expectations—and then He doesn't answer our prayers questioning His motives and governance. Because most of us are rejected at our core, we project that rejection on to God and believe that He is rejecting us, when—in fact—we are rejecting Him. ***This is where we start to wander in the self-made wilderness of grumbling!*** We walk around murmuring, complaining, muttering to ourselves against God, because we believe that He has **not** lived up to His part of the bargain. We have lived up to our part of the bargain. We have done all the religious things that God asks, so God should give us what we believe we are entitled to: a mate, a better mate, a different mate, a car, a house, better children, a healing, a better job, popularity, prestige, a leadership position at church, etc.

I don't believe that most of us are aware of our grumbling, because we are religiously sophisticated enough **not** to grumble directly against God. Instead, we are full of negative murmuring about our lives and often the things of God. We are too smart to say what we feel clearly or aloud, but don't realize that God can decipher our grumbling.

The next thing you know, something is wrong with everything. We can see the negative side of everything. ***This negativity is a deadly, contagious disease that infects and corrupts everything and everyone around us!***

***Now, when this grumbling is allowed to defile everything and everyone, it degenerates into a mindset of hopelessness.***

***Please hear my heart loved ones! I ache and cry over the hopelessness that I see and sense among believers! God has a better destiny for us!***

So, how can we break this stronghold and stop the ravages of rejection?

Praise! Praise is a means of taking back territory from the devil! ***However, we underestimate the power of choice (victors) and overestimate the limits of God's sovereignty (victims)! Make a choice!***

Let's talk about a specific kind of praise: thanksgiving!

***Do you know that thanksgiving is praise?*** Thanksgiving is praising God for what He has done! Worship is primarily giving God the glory that His name is due, either verbally or non-verbally, but praise is verbal acclaim of the Person or acts of God. ***Thanksgiving, again, is***

*verbally acclaiming or praising God for what He has done!*

There are seven major words in the Old Testament for praise. I want to deal with two of those words that are connected to thanksgiving. The first Hebrew word is

> yadah 3034 *yaw-daw'* "literally to *use* (i.e. hold out) *the hand*; physically to *throw* (a stone, an arrow) at or away; especially to *revere* or *worship* (with extended hands)" (*Strong's Greek & Hebrew Dictionary*).

Therefore, this word evidently means to worship God with raised hands!

This word is often translated "to give thanks." One of the most common phrases of the Old Testament is **"give thanks** to the LORD for He is good and His lovingkindness is forever" (1 Chron. 16:34; Psalm 106:1; 107:1; 118:1; 118:29, 136:1; 136:29).

This phrase can be translated, "Praise God through the lifting of your hands for He is good and His loving kindness is forever!"

Let's make **the choice** to cultivate a lifestyle and practice of giving thanks to God, through raising our hands! We must come to understand that we should use everything that we are, body, soul, and spirit, to praise God!

This perspective is beautifully captured in

> Lamentations 3:41 (NASB-U), "We lift up our heart and hands Toward God in heaven."

This is also stated in the New Testament. It is captured in Paul's words to His son in the Gospel, Timothy. Paul wrote in

> 1 Timothy 2:8 (NASB-U), "Therefore I want the men in every place to pray, lifting up holy hands, without wrath and dissension."

There was probably something going on in the church at Ephesus that caused Paul to say this to the men. Nevertheless, we can extend Paul's desire to all who gather in worship. **Let us learn** *to praise and thank God by raising our hands! This will stop us from grumbling against God.*

## Thankfulness Transforms

In the early days of the settlement of the West, travelers encountered considerable difficulty. One party of pioneers on the Oregon Trail had suffered greatly from a scarcity of water and grass. Some of the wagons had broken down, causing delays in the stifling heat. Along with these adverse circumstances came a general feeling of fretfulness. Optimism and cheer were gone. One night a meeting was called for the purpose of airing their complaints. When they had gathered around the campfire, one of them arose and said, "Before we do anything else, I think we should first thank God that we have come this far with no loss of life, with no serious trouble from the Indians, and that we have enough strength left to finish our journey." After the prayer, there was silence. No one had any grievances that they felt were important enough to voice. *Thankfulness often transforms a grumbling spirit into one of contentment, enabling us to see the many mercies of God that we ordinarily would overlook.*

Let's deal with the second Hebrew word that has to do with thanksgiving.

> todah 8426 *to-daw'* "from Hebrew 3034 (yadah); properly an *extension* of the hand, i.e. (by implication) *avowal*, or (usually) *adoration*; specifically a *choir* of worshippers :- confession, **to give the sacrifice of praise**, **thanks (-giving, offering)**" (*Strong's Greek & Hebrew Dictionary*).

This Hebrew word is, in fact, a derivative of the first word that we covered, and it means to extend the hand as a sacrifice of praise or thanks. Yes, to raise our hands is a sacrifice of praise! ***It's a personal sacrifice to ignore our pride and lift our hands in Church. Jack Hayford said that two things confront our pride like nothing else: praise and tongues!***

***We each have an internal policeman, who has been educated and authorized by our culture to stop us from having genuine spiritual experiences!***

Consequently, it is lifting of the hands in thanksgiving that will smash holes through the stronghold of negativity and grumbling, so that you can get to God and God can get to you!

Therefore, let's make Psalm 100:4, where this word is used, our practice.

> Psalm 100:4 (NASB), "Enter His gates with thanksgiving (*todah*, i.e. lifting our hands in thanks), And His courts with praise (*tehillah*, i.e. a song of praise). Give thanks (*yadah*, i.e. lifting our hands in praise) to Him; bless (*barak*, i.e. to bless by kneeling) His name" (*explanations added*).

# Chapter 5

# Rejection Distorts our Discernment of God's Destiny

## The Certainty of The Unseen

In his book *Daily Gems*, Dwight L. Moody commented about the breath-taking beauty of the Alps. He said that "houses of faraway villages can be seen with great distinctness, so that sometimes the number of panes of glass in a...window can be counted. The distance looks so short that the place to which the traveler is journeying appears almost at hand. This is because of the clearness of the atmosphere." Moody then drew the following spiritual analogy: "We sometimes dwell in high altitudes of grace, and Heaven seems very near....

*At other times the cloud and fog, caused by suffering and sin, cut off our sight. Our perception is distorted.* However, we are as near Heaven in the one case as we are in the other, and we are just as sure of gaining it."

*The next listed effect of rejection in Deuteronomy 1:26-33 is a distorted discernment of God's destiny.* This is seen in the words

> "He has brought us out of the land of
> Egypt to deliver us into the hands of
> the Amorites to destroy us."

When I was writing the sermons that I'm using in this book, I was unaware of how many Saints don't understand destiny. So, let's take the time to define the word.

> **Destiny** is the positive purpose and
> end that God sets out for the lives of
> His children that they work towards
> with Him, through the power of the
> Holy Spirit.

- Destiny is positive!
- Destiny is the positive purpose (reason for existence)!
- Destiny is the positive end (goal)!
- Destiny is the positive purpose and goal that God sets out or presents to His children for their lives.
- God's children must work toward their destiny, with God!
- Destiny is worked toward, with God, through power of the Holy Spirit.
- Destiny, evidently, is **not** guaranteed, but depends upon our choices in prayer, Bible reading, Bible study, obeying the Word of God, fellowshipping with the Saints, godly suffering, etc.
- Destiny is **not** negative!
- Destiny is **not** a fate, which one has **no** power to affect or change!

God did **not** deliver the Children of Israel out of the bondage of Egypt to deliver them into the hands of their enemies for destruction! *Their destiny was the Promised Land.* Living in the Promised Land was the purpose and end that

God set out for them hundreds of years earlier, through Abraham, and that they were to work towards with God, through His miraculous power.

Yet, the first generation of Israelites did **not** make it into the Promised Land, because of their choices. However, the second generation did make it into the Promised Land, because of their choices. ***Destiny is the unsearchable, inscrutable working together of Man's free will and God's sovereignty!***

Did the children of Israel know about God's destiny for them? Clearly! Then, how were they deceived? They were spiritually deceived! They were intellectually aware of God's destiny for them, but they could **not *spiritually discern***, grasp, or believe in that destiny.

> ***Spiritual discernment is the ability to detect something with spiritual senses or faculties.***

The necessary faculties for discerning God's destiny are **not *cerebral***, but ***spiritual***. Moses explained this to the Children of Israel in

Deuteronomy 29:2-6, "And Moses summoned all Israel and said to them, 'You have seen all that the LORD did before your eyes in the land of Egypt to Pharaoh and all his servants and all his land; the great trials which your eyes have seen, those great signs and wonders. **Yet to this day the Lord has not given you a heart to know, nor eyes to see, nor ears to hear.** And I have led you forty years in the wilderness; your clothes have not worn out on you, and your sandal has not worn out on your foot. You have not eaten bread, nor have you drunk wine or strong drink, in order that you might know that I am the LORD your God" (*bold type added*).

Consequently, the question arises, "What is God talking about?" They certainly had ***physical*** hearts, eyes, and ears! Therefore, God must be talking about their ***spiritual*** hearts, eyes, and ears. God had **not** given them the spiritual faculties to perceive what was going on! ***They had neither spiritual knowledge, nor spiritual*** *discernment.* Why? *It wasn't because God didn't want them to know, see, and hear, but because these spiritual faculties had been damaged through "the ravages of rejection."*

*How could they be held accountable for discerning something that Moses plainly states that God had not given them the faculties to discern?* Well, Moses is only talking about God's part in **not** giving the Israelites this discernment. However, in the passage before us, we can see that God did not give them this spiritual discernment, because of their grumbling, lack of trust, disobedience, etc., etc., etc.

Moreover, lack of discernment is not simply psychological, it is a satanic stronghold that came from the demonic ravages of rejection, when they were down in Egypt.

Edgardo Silvoso of Harvest Evangelism gives this definition of a stronghold:

"a stronghold is a mindset impregnated with hopelessness that causes the believer to accept as unchangeable something that he/she knows is contrary to the will of God."[1]

[1] Edgardo Silvoso, taken from a memorandum to supporters and friends on "Plan Resistencia," September 15, 1990: p. 3.

The Israelites knew that conquering the Promised Land was God's will for them, but their mindset was impregnated with hopelessness, which caused them to accept their inability to enter the Promised Land as unchangeable!

Let's apply this truth to ourselves. I know that many modern people can't handle the truth, but the truth of the matter is that many believers in Jesus, have a mindset that is impregnated with hopelessness when it comes to their destiny. There is a seed of hopelessness that has been planted in their minds, and large trees can grow from small seeds. This seed grows imperceptibly, until it chokes and obliterates God's destiny in them. I run into many Christians who feel that God hates them and couldn't possibly have anything positive for them in the future. They don't understand why God even puts up with them. This saddens me, because the real reason for their hopelessness is the ravages of rejection. ***They have a destiny, but they don't have the spiritual perception to discern it!***

In this book, we are working on only one answer to the problem of rejection: praise! When we praise God, we are speaking words that cause us to reevaluate our perception of God.

Moreover, reevaluating God will bring about a reevaluation of everything else, and that certainly includes our evaluation of our destiny.

Furthermore, praise also grows new spiritual faculties. The more we praise God, the more our spiritual discernment of Him will grow. Then we can use that spiritual discernment to zero in on our destiny.

Let's add a new set of Bible verses to our glossary on praise.

Isaiah 42:10-13, "Sing to the LORD a new song, ***sing His praise*** from the end of the earth! You who go down to the sea, and all that is in it. You islands and those who dwell on them. Let the wilderness and its cities lift up their voices, the settlements where Kedar inhabits. Let the inhabitants of Sela sing aloud, let them shout for joy from the tops of the mountains. Let them give glory to the LORD, and **declare His praise** in the coastlands. The LORD will go forth like a warrior, He will arouse His zeal like a man of war. He will utter a shout, yes, He will raise a war cry. He will prevail against His **enemies**."

The word that is translated "praise" two times is tehillah.

tehilah 8416 *teh-hil law'* "from Hebrew 1984 (halal); *laudation*; specifically (concrete) a *hymn* :- praise" (*Strong's Greek & Hebrew Dictionary*). **A song containing praise, a hymn.** To glory. Used of Temple worship in choir, or organized praise in the midst of the congregation.

This word occurs 49 times in the KJV. "Intercession for someone, supplication, a hymn (Isaiah 56:7)."[10]

This word is from the same Hebrew root which is translated "hallelujah." ***We need to sing a new song of hallelujah unto God!*** Did you see what happens when they sang "hallelujah" to God? ***It aroused God!*** It aroused God's warrior zeal. He got up and went forth like the Warrior that He is. He began to shout in heaven and raise a war cry. Then He prevailed against His enemies.

***Therefore, when we sing "hallelujah" to God, it arouses Him and his warrior zeal. He gets up, goes forth like a Warrior, begins to shout in heaven and raise a war cry. Then He prevails against his enemies, which are also our enemies. God begins to smite the enemies of our destiny!*** He begins to slay the demons who distort our discernment of His destiny and free our spirits and minds to a Spirit-appraised, Spirit-discerned destiny! Our destiny is spiritual and it can only be discerned with spiritual faculties!

---

[10] Cindy Jacobs, *Possessing The Gates Of The Enemy*, Baker Book House, Grand Rapids, Michigan, seventh printing 1998, p. 182.

I have come to doubt that God ever responds violently. ***Therefore, when we sing "halle-lujah" to God, it arouses Him to move on our behalf, by abandoning our enemies.*** This causes demons and enemies of our destruction to destroy themselves!

To discuss this doubt would take us too far afield of our present subject.

So, start singing songs of praise to God and watch Him destroy the enemies of your destiny!

Right now, I am asking God to give you a super-natural discernment, so that you can see your des-tiny—if just for a moment. If you are a believer in Jesus, the Christ, your destiny is stated in:

> Romans 8:28, "And we know that God causes all things to work together for good to those who love God, to those who are called according to His purpose."

Let's break down the words of this verse.
***"We know."***

The Greek word for "know" means "to see or perceive and hence to come to know." Remember that this kind of knowledge must be discerned through the Holy Spirit, but is often blocked by the destructive effects of rejection. Our perception needs to be based on spiritual faculties that transcend the physical faculties of sight, smell, taste, touch, and hearing. Those of us who are Spirit-filled and Spirit-controlled spiritually *know or perceive* what God is doing.

**"...that God causes all things to work together for good..."**

This does **not** mean that "all things" will make you happy, fulfill your desires, exempt you from suffering, etc., etc., etc. This means that "all things" will ultimately eventuate in you entering the Promised Land of victory and reigning with Christ. ***The word "good" represents our positive end and God's glory!*** Somebody praise God in here!

***But there are two sides of this equation.***

- There is the human side and there is the divine side.
- There is our side and there is God's side.
- There is human will and there is divine sovereignty.

Man's side of this equation is captured in the words

**"...to those who love God..."**

We cooperate with the destiny that God has set before us, by loving God with *agape* love. **This is the divine love that is produced in the heart of a yielded Christian through the power of the Holy Spirit.** So, even though this is our responsibility, it cannot be fulfilled except through the power of the Holy Spirit. This means loving God with all our emotions, all our intellect, all our choices, and all our physical vitality. This means loving God wholeheartedly or with all that we are.

God's side of this equation is captured in the words

**"...to those who are called according to His purpose."**

Now, the words purpose and destiny are synonyms. So, let's substitute the word "destiny" in

> Romans 8:28, "And we know that God causes all things to work together for good to those who love God, to those who are called according to His **_destiny_**" (*bold type and underlining is added*).

God has a purpose or destiny for every person that He calls! God has a positive purpose and end that He sets out for the lives of His children! *Moreover, God is bent on working with us to give us this destiny!*

*Now, the question comes to bear, "Whom does God call?"* "Call," in this sense, represents the upward call of God that is available to every person that He calls or effectively invites to salvation. In short, every believer is "called according to God's purpose or destiny for him/her."

Now, when did God give us this destiny? Paul tells Timothy in

> 2 Timothy 1:9, "Who has saved us, and called us with a holy calling, not according to our works, but according to His own purpose and grace which was granted us in Christ Jesus from all eternity."

*He gave it to us <u>in time</u> when we responded to His call of salvation, but He gave it to us <u>in eternity past</u>, in Jesus, the Christ!*

The word purpose is

*prothesis 4286*; from Greek (*protithemi*); *a setting forth,* i.e. figurative *proposal,* specifically *the showbread, sacred* (bread) :- consecrated(3), purpose(7), resolute(m)(1), sacred(1).[11]

This is fascinating! ***This word is also translated "showbread," in the New Testament.*** God has consecrated and set forth a purpose for us before Himself and before us. This setting forth is like the setting forth of the shewbread or the bread of presence, in the Tabernacle, before the Ark of the Covenant, i.e. before the face of God.

So, in what way is our purpose like the setting forth of the bread of the presence before God's face?

"In Exodus 25:30, the LORD's instructions concerning the paraphernalia of worship include a provision that bread be kept always on a table set before the Holy of Holies. This bread was called the bread of presence, or shewbread. The literal meaning of the Hebrew expression is 'bread of the face.' It consisted of twelve loaves of presumably unleavened bread, and it was replaced each Sabbath" (*Holman Bible Dictionary*, James A.

---

[11] NASB Greek Dictionary.

Brooks.) Certainly, this bread was "a type of Christ as the Bread of Life, the sustainer of each individual believer-priest" (*Unger's Bible Dictionary*), but it represented even more. "The number of the loaves represented the twelve tribes of Israel, and also the entire spiritual Israel, "the true Israel;" and the placing of them on the table symbolized the entire consecration of Israel to the LORD, and their acceptance of God as their God" (*Easton's Bible Dictionary*). ***This symbolizes Israel and her destiny, being set apart constantly before the face or presence of God! This also represents spiritual Israel, the spiritual seed of Abraham, i.e. the Church of Jesus, the Christ.***

***God has placed the proposal of our destiny before us, and more importantly, before Himself where He can watch over it constantly. By implication, since the destiny is inside of us, He has placed us before His omni-present watchful eye to fulfill our destiny.***

***That is another reason to sing praise to His name!***

God has a plan for your life! If you want to continue to discern that destiny, continue to sing songs of praise to God and you'll discern God fighting for your destiny!

Chapter 6

# Rejection Makes Us Susceptible to Negative Reports

## Our Unseen Helpers

At one point in Martin Luther's stormy career, with the forces of Church and state already against him, he received some additional bad news from friends. His reply to that report went something like this: "Recently I have been looking up at the night sky, spangled and studded with stars, and I found no pillars to hold them up. Yet they did not fall." The great reformer had been encouraged by God's unseen power in the heavens. ***Therefore, he was not shaken by negative reports.***

*The next listed effect of rejection in Deuteronomy 1:26-33 is susceptibility to negative reports.* The negative report came from ten of the twelve spies that were sent into the Promised Land on a spy mission. They went up to spy out the land and see if it was all that God said it was. Ten of them came back with a negative report. Only Joshua and Caleb gave a positive report. These statistics are probably indicative of what you will find today. *You won't find many people who are positive.* The clear majority of people in this world are focused on the negative, rather than the positive. *So, if you find a positive person, hang <u>on</u> to him/her and hang <u>with</u> him or her!*

Two boys illustrate the difference between those who are fixated on the negative and those who are fixated on the positive.

## Thorns or Roses?

While eating some grapes, one of the lads remarked, "Aren't they sweet?" "I guess so," the other replied, "but they're full of seeds."

Wandering into a garden, one of them exclaimed, "Look at those big, beautiful red roses!" The other commented, "They're full of thorns!"

It was a warm day, so they stopped at the store for a soft drink. After several swallows, the one youngster complained, "My bottle's half-empty already." The other quickly responded, "Mine's still half-full!"

*I want to cultivate and hang with people who see life from a positive perspective.* God is doing something miraculous and wonderful in our church right now, but all that some people can see is the negatives.

The negative report of the ten spies contains three perceptions:

1. The people are bigger and taller than us.
2. The cities are large and fortified to heaven.
3. The sons of the Anakim are there.

*The bottom line of the negative report was, "We have <u>no</u> chance of obtaining the Promised Land, because of the obstacles!"* The way that they perceived these obstacles is interesting indeed. They saw the people who occupied the Promised Land as bigger and taller than they were. ***Therefore, they didn't believe they could defeat them.***

Nevertheless, they didn't stop there. Their perception of the cities of Canaan, which composed the Promised Land, was that the cities were large and fortified to heaven. ***Notice the hyperbole.*** The cities weren't just fortified, they were fortified to heaven! How do you attack and get into a city with fortifications or walls that reach all the way to heaven? ***You don't!***

However, they went even further. They pointed out that the sons of the Anakim were there. The sons of the Anakim were giants. Not only were the people bigger and taller than they were, but the people were from a renowned race of giants. How do you beat a renowned race of giants? ***You don't!***

***This is a thoroughly negative report. Nevertheless, what brought about this negative report? The impact of slavery and the rejection that they received down in Egypt had so damaged them that they brought back a negative report.***

Now, this negative report kept the children of Israel from trusting God, obeying God, and advancing into the Promised Land of their inheritance and destiny. The negative report was the last straw. Four hundred years of slavery had dampened their enthusiasm concerning Jehovah God. The negative report put their fire out with respect to trusting God to give them the Promised Land. ***The Ravages of Rejection made them susceptible to this negative report.***

***Consequently, they refused to enter the Promised Land and were made to wander in the wilderness for 40 years, until every adult disbeliever died!***

Since we are covering these ravages of rejection as strongholds, please allow me to remind you of the definition that we are using. Edgardo Silvoso of Harvest Evangelism gives this definition of a stronghold:

> "a stronghold is a mindset impregnated with hopelessness that causes the believer to accept as unchangeable something that he/she knows is contrary to the will of God."[1]

[1] Edgardo Silvoso, taken from a memorandum to supporters and friends on "Plan Resistencia," September 15, 1990: p. 3.

91

Here are some questions to help you apply this information to yourself.

- Are you susceptible to negative reports?
- Do people telling you what you can't do stop you from attempting great things for God?
- Do people telling you the odds stop you from doing what you know God wants you to do?
- Has rejection impregnated your mind with hopelessness with respect to your destiny in the Promised Land of victorious, abundant Christian living?
- Has this mindset become a stronghold that causes you to accept as unchangeable your defeated position, even though you know that this defeated position is contrary to the will of God?

*Let's talk about one area of life that has us defeated, dethroned, and hopeless because of negative reports.* *The area I am talking about is addictions.*

God wants us to begin to reign in this life with Him. He does **not** want anything else in life mastering us. God wants us to live in the Promised Land of freedom. Jesus said to some Jews who had believed in Him, "You shall know the truth and the truth shall set you free." Yet, America is a nation full of addicted people.

We are addicted to pornography.
We are addicted to sex.
We are addicted to relationships.
   Intellectual adultery.
   Emotional adultery.
   Spiritual adultery.

We are addicted to adrenaline.
We are addicted to anger.
We are addicted to shopping.
We are addicted to 1-900 numbers.
We are addicted to all kinds of substances.
   Alcohol.
   Illegal drugs.
   Marijuana.
   Cocaine.
   Crack.
   Ecstasy.
   Etc.
   Legal or prescription drugs.
   Pain pills.

Sleeping pills.

Diet pills.

Etc.

Food.

Alcoholics.

Potato chip junkies.

Chocolate bingers.

Pop guzzlers.

Heroin.

Meth.

Etc.

*Addictions are giants who live in cities that are fortified to heaven!*

*So, how do we deal with these giants? How do we overcome our susceptibility to negative reports?*

First, we need to change our attitude. Let me illustrate.

## Giant Problems

A shoe salesman was sent to a remote part of the country. When he arrived, he was dismayed because everyone went around barefooted. So, he wired the company, "No prospect of sales. People don't wear shoes here." Later another salesman went to the same territory. He too immediately sent word to the home office. However, his telegram read, "Great potential! People don't wear shoes here!"

***Here we see two different attitudes about the same situation!***

***So, obstacles are opportunities to trust God for a miracle!***

- When Satan tells you that you will never get out of the clutches of alcohol, this is an opportunity to trust God for a miracle!
- When Satan tells you that you will never get off of drugs, this is an opportunity to trust God for a miracle!
- When Satan tells you that you will never stop going to peep shows, this is an opportunity to trust God for a miracle?
- When Satan tells you that you will never be able to discipline yourself to eat right, this is an opportunity to trust God for a miracle!
- When Satan tells you that you will never stop spending and get out of debt, this is an opportunity to trust God for a miracle!

When I organized the church that I pastor, I did despite negative reports that said I could **not** succeed! I was told that I was not dynamic enough to start a church. I was told that I had no backing and could not start a church. However, I didn't know enough to let negative reports change my attitude.

This brings us to a very important question, "How do we break the stronghold of rejection that makes us susceptible to negative reports?"

The answer is captured in the phrase: "Praise is a means of taking territory back from the devil." We want to work on this statement by adding another Scripture to our glossary of Scriptures on praise.

> Psalm 8:1-2, "For the choir director; on the Gittith. A Psalm of David. O LORD, our Lord, how majestic is Thy name in all the earth, who hast displayed Thy splendor above the heavens! From the mouth of infants and nursing babes Thou hast established strength, because of Thine adversaries, to make the enemy and the revengeful cease."

Now you are probably thinking, "What does these verses have to do with praise? The word 'praise' does **not** even occur in the verse?" Well, this is where knowledge of the original languages becomes instructive. The Hebrew word that is translated "strength" is

> `oz, *oze*; or (fully) **owz**, oze; from Hebrew 5810 (`azaz); *strength* in various applications (*force, security, majesty, praise*) :- boldness, loud, might, power, strength, strong (*The NASB Dictionary*).

However, this word can be translated "praise." In fact, it is translated that way in the NIV.

> Psalm 8:1-2 (NIV), "For the director of music. According to gittith. A psalm of David. O LORD, our Lord, how majestic is your name in all the earth! You have set your glory above the heavens. From the lips of children and infants you have **ordained praise** because of

your enemies, to silence the foe and the avenger" (*bold type added*).

***Hallelujah! God ordained praise from the lips of children and infants because of His enemies.*** Through the praise of children and infants, God silences the foe and the avenger. Why praise from children and infants? ***Because children and infants are innocent, trusting, and free with their emotions. Children easily offer wholehearted praise. It is <u>not</u> so with adults!***

Jack Hayford said that there are two things that confront human pride: praise and tongues. However, we are discussing praise. ***To praise God, we must confront our pride and become like children!***

Jesus quoted this same verse in the New Testament. After Jesus made a whip and cleansed the Temple of the moneychangers, Jesus healed the lame and blind in that same Temple. When the chief priests and scribes saw the wonderful things that Jesus had done and the children crying out,

"Hosanna to the Son of David,"

they became indignant and said Him,

"Do you hear what these (*children*) are saying?"

"Hosanna" means "Save, we pray." It is an exclamation of adoration or praise. ***The chief priests and scribes were angry about the praise that the children were exclaiming.*** It was in this situation, in the 16<sup>th</sup> verse of the 21<sup>st</sup> chapter of Matthew, that Jesus quotes Psalm 8:2. He said to the chief priests and scribes,

> "Yes; have you never read, 'Out of the mouth of infants and nursing babes Thou hast prepared praise for Thyself'?"

***Here Jesus also translates the Hebrew word in Psalm 8:2 as "praise." God uses the praise of infants and nursing babes against his enemies to silence the foe and the avenger.*** God's enemies are our enemies, so we need to get infants and nursing babes to praise Him. Right? Well, let's look at one more Scripture.

On one occasion when the disciples asked Jesus about who was greatest in the kingdom of heaven, Jesus said in

> Matthew 18:3, "And said, 'Truly I say to you, unless you are converted and

The Ravages of **Rejection**

become like children, you shall not enter the kingdom of heaven.'"

*Jesus wanted His disciples to become like children, and likewise I believe He wants us to become like children and to praise Him like children. When we praise God like children, He will use that praise against our enemies. He will silence our foes and avengers and reduce our susceptibility to negative reports.*

*<u>Children who praise their fathers are secure in their love and hardly susceptible to negative reports</u>!*

If you want to make yourself less susceptible to negative reports, praise God like a child!

# Chapter 7

# Rejection Perverts Our Perception of Ourselves

## Looking into God's Mirror

The noted Christian physician A. T. Schofield told of sitting with some friends in a hotel lobby lined with mirrors. As he glanced at one of them, he noticed a group of people some distance away seated around another table. Being near-sighted, he could not tell what they were doing, but he observed one person in particular with an unfriendly expression on his face that he didn't like. The man was looking in the direction of Schofield and seemed to be listening to their discussion. Annoyed by this suspicious character, he suggested to his companions, "Let's not speak so loudly; those folks over there are sure to hear us." Immediately his friends burst out laughing, for the doctor had really been seeing his own image reflected in one of the large mirrors on the wall.

The doctor saw a perverted image of himself. *How often is our image of ourselves perverted?*

Remember: we are looking at the destructive effects of rejection in Deuteronomy 1:26-33. Now, the entire story is not given there, because Moses is simply reviewing the history for the people before He commissions them again and then dies. *However, the negative report of the ten spies precipitated a perverted perception concerning themselves.* That perverted perception is recorded in

> Numbers 13:33 (NASB-U), "There also we saw the Nephilim (the sons of Anak are part of the Nephilim); and we became like grasshoppers in our own sight, and so we were in their sight."

*Notice the wording.* It doesn't say that they became as grasshoppers in the sight of their enemies, but in their own sight. Then it goes on to say,

"...and so we were in their sight."

### Their perception of themselves was perverted and pessimistic!

- Being **pessimistic** is expecting the worse to happen in every situation.

  I tend **not** to be pessimistic. *Pessimism is very close to hopelessness!*

- Being **optimistic** is taking a hopeful and positive view of future outcomes.

  I am optimistic about the future outcome of my destiny.

- Being **realistic** is seeking what is achievable or possible, based on known facts.

  I am generally realistic about most things.

*Pessimism is one of the major impacts of rejection!*

*Notice also that the Nephilim saw them in the same way that they saw themselves.* They somehow projected their self-image in such a way that their enemies received the projection and also believed it!

We project our own negative perceptions onto the screens of people around us! They watch the horror movie and begin to believe it also.

The devil often moves boldly into our lives and situations, because he perceives and receives the negative self-image that we are projecting into the atmosphere!

*Their perception of themselves was also in direct inverse proportion to how they viewed their enemy, i.e. the bigger they saw their enemies; the smaller they saw themselves. Moreover, vice versa, the smaller they saw their enemies; the bigger they saw themselves.*

This is sad, because their perception of themselves **shouldn't** have been affected by their perception of their enemies. Their perception of themselves should have been based upon How

God saw them. ***They were not <u>puny grasshop-</u>
<u>pers</u>; they were <u>prophesied giant-killers</u>!***

- I refuse to let pessimism keep me from
  accepting my own perception of myself.

Paul said in

> 1 Corinthians 4:3-4 (NASB-U), "But to
> me it is a very small thing that I may
> be examined by you, or by any human
> court; In fact, I do not even examine
> myself. [4] For I am conscious of
> nothing against myself, yet I am not by
> this acquitted; but the one who exam-
> ines me is the Lord."

- I doubly refuse to accept the distorted perceptions of others about me!
- I seek to see myself as God sees me.

David prayed in

> Psalm 139:23-24 (NLT), "Search me, O
> God, and know my heart; test me and
> know my thoughts. Point out anything

in me that offends you, and lead me along the path of everlasting life."

In applying these truths to ourselves, we have been considering strongholds. Edgardo Silvoso of Harvest Evangelism gives this definition of a stronghold:

> "a stronghold is a mindset impregnated with hopelessness that causes the believer to accept as unchangeable something that he/she knows is contrary to the will of God."[1]
>
> ---
> [1]  Edgardo Silvoso, taken from a memorandum to supporters and friends on "Plan Resistencia," September 15, 1990: p. 3.

Where in our lives do we have a mindset impregnated with hopeless that causes us to accept as unchangeable something that God wants us to do because of how we see ourselves, when we know that the situation is contrary to the will of God?

Well, let's stay right where we are. We battle for the same thing that the Children of Israel battled for, i.e. victory over our enemies.

***A major enemy for men is sexual lust.*** When we get saved we believe that our lust is taken care of. Consequently, we are often startled and frightened when we realize that, although our souls are saved, we still have a major battle with lust. This is complicated by the fact that most men, even leaders, are unwilling to honestly and openly talk about lust. Consequently, we feel that we are all alone struggling with this mortal enemy of our souls.

Lust, particularly as it is manifested in the area of pornography, is a major giant in America. ***Pornography is eating the men of America alive!*** By the grace of God, I have been kept from hard-core porn, but I have my own struggles with lust. ***Nevertheless, I doubt that anyone in America can escape soft porn, if s/he watches TV.***

Added to this whole struggle is the fact that the majority report is that lust is bigger than we are and uncontrollable. Therefore, it is fortified against any attempts to conquer it, and it is a renowned giant.

Moreover, we project to others around us that we are helpless in the face of this giant!

*Therefore, because of rejection, we are susceptible to negative perceptions of ourselves! When we accept our slavery to lust as unchangeable, it has a definite degrading impact upon our self-image and the estimate of our worth!*

*A major enemy for many women is bitterness that comes from <u>not</u> forgiving insensitive or abusive men.* Although the bitterness may never be dealt with directly or overtly, it often lurks just beneath the surface of consciousness and colors everything that these women deal with. *I am running into more and more women, who because of the movement of the Lord in this church, are becoming aware of the fact that although they thought they had worked through their bitterness against men—that bitterness had simply been pushed down, submerged, suppressed, or repressed.* It is **not** a pleasant thing to become aware of bitterness in your life, but bitterness is a cancer that will eventually destroy you—if it is **not** dealt with!

Added to this whole struggle is the fact that the majority report is that bitterness is bigger than we are, it is fortified against any attempts to conquer it, and it is a renowned giant. ***The report is that bitterness can't be conquered, and even if it can be conquered it isn't worth the time or effort.***

Moreover, women often project that bitterness to everyone around them, including the enemy who will use it as a base of attack!

Therefore, because of rejection, bitterness, and unforgiveness, many women have a perverted perception of themselves! They know that God does not want them wallowing in the burrow of bitterness, but they can't seem to get up. Consequently, their self-image is very low.

***This may be a contributing factor to a rise in lesbianism, i.e. a pessimistic outlook on life that seeks in women what it cannot find in men!***

So, how do we change this perverted perception of ourselves?

***First, I believe we must work more on the root of the problem than on the fruit of the problem.*** If we want to kill an apple tree, knocking all of the apples off the tree is **not** enough. We have to do something to the root system of the tree. Simply trying to change a negative perception of ourselves won't stop the thing that is producing the negative perception.

We need to work on our incorrect perception of God; which will help us recover from the ravages of rejection; which will affect our perception of our enemies; which will affect our perception of ourselves. How do we do that? ***Through praise!***

I think David captured it best in

> Psalm 34:3 (NASB-U), "O magnify the LORD with me, And let us exalt His name together."

This was **not** written to priests, but to the rag-tag group of distressed, in debt, and discontented men who gathered to David, while he was running from King Saul! David exhorted those around him to join him in magnifying, enlarging, or making YHWH (*the covenant name of God with*

*Israel which they refused to pronounce)* larger, through praise! When they praised YHWH and exalted His name, He grew bigger. Now, we know that God doesn't get bigger in reality, but He gets bigger to the worshipers and praisers.

***These men became mighty men of valor and the officers of David's royal court, when his reign was established!***

***Consequently, if we make God large through praise, our perception of God will change.*** When our perception of God changes and He becomes large, our enemies will look much smaller. This will affect our perception of God, our perception of our enemies, and our perception of ourselves. We will see God more accurately. We will see our enemies more accurately. Moreover, we will see ourselves more accurately.

Now, I am **not** suggesting that this will automatically cure all our battles with lust and bitterness. ***I am suggesting it is hard to even get into the battle, until we get some of our perceptions straightened out, and this begins with praise!***

- Lust won't look as large and invincible, when God is magnified!

111

- Bitterness won't look as large and invincible, when God is magnified!

***Then we will stop projecting to people around us and to our demonic enemies that we are worth nothing.*** We will begin to project faith in the great God that we serve. We will begin to project to others

> Philippians 4:13 (NASB-U), "I can do all things through Him who strengthens me."

This is **not** arrogance, but self-confidence through God-confidence!

We want to affirm this statement again by adding another Scripture to our glossary of Scriptures on praise.

> Psalm 149:5-9 (NASB), "⁵ Let the godly ones exult in glory; Let them sing for joy on their beds. ⁶ *Let* the high praises of God *be* in their mouth, And a two-edged sword in their hand, ⁷ To execute vengeance on the nations And punishment

on the peoples, [8] To bind their kings
with chains And their nobles with fetters of iron, [9] To execute on them the
judgment written; This is an honor for
all His godly ones. Praise the LORD! "

I only want to extract the truth of verse six (6).
***This paragraph of Scripture starts out with
a picture of God's Saints exulting or greatly
rejoicing in God's glory, or magnifying God.***
David exhorts the Saints to sing for joy on their
beds. However, they don't stay in bed. In the next
verse, they are in battle. Life certainly has its battles. In fact, according to verse six (6), the lives
of the Saints often consist of worship and warfare, celebration and combat, praise and battle.
***However, there is also another couplet here:
praise and power. David exhorts the Saints to
let the high praises of God be in their mouths
and a two-edged sword in their hand.***
C. H. Spurgeon, records the following words of
William Taylor, in *The Treasury Of David*, "Praise
and power go ever hand in hand. The two things
act and react upon each other. An era of spiritual force in the Church is always one of praise;

and when there comes some grand outburst of sacred song, we may expect that the people of God are entering upon some new crusade for Christ. **He who has a 'new song in his mouth' is ever stronger to wage war, than the man who has a dumb spirit and a hymnless heart"** (*bold type added*).

*Praise and power go together!* As these Saints went to battle with the enemies of God, they did so with *high praises* in their mouth and a two-edged sword in their hand. What does the two-edged sword represent but the Bible and the willingness to do battle? *Nevertheless, what do the high praises in their mouths represent? The Hebrew word means the exaltation or extolling praises of God. What is this, but the magnification of God?* As we go to battle with the enemies of lust and bitterness, let us do so with the *high praises* of God in our mouths, the Bible in our hands and hearts, and a willingness to do conflict with the enemies of God and the enemies of our soul that God might be glorified.

Moreover, God will bless us with what is an honor for all of the Saints:

• To execute vengeance on the nations;

Every nation that comes against God's people shall be avenged, when we battle with high praises and the two-edged sword of the Word of God, in our hands!

- To execute punishment on the peoples;

  Every people that comes against God shall be punished, when we battle with high praises and the two-edged sword of the Word of God, in our hands!

- To bind their kings with chains;

  The kings of enemy nations and powers will be bound, when we battle with high praises and the two-edged sword of the Word of God, in our hands!

- To bind their nobles with fetters of iron;

  The nobles of enemy nations and powers will be bound, when we battle with high

praises and the two-edged sword of the
Word of God, in our hands!

- To execute on them the judgment written.

The judgment of Jehovah shall be pub-
licly written on all His enemies, because
we go to battle with the high praises on
our lips and the two-edged sword of the
Word of God, in our hands.

What is David talking about but power and
complete victory over the enemies of Jehovah
God! *Likewise, when we magnify God and face
His enemies with the two-edged sword of the
Word of God, He will honor us by giving us
power and using us to bring complete victory
over His enemies and ours!*

# Chapter 8

# Rejection Makes Us Susceptible to Negative Emotions

## Friend or Foe?

During the Boer War (1899-1902), a man was convicted of a very unusual crime. He was found guilty of being a "discourager." The South African town of Ladysmith was under attack, and this traitor would move up and down the lines of soldiers who were defending the city and do everything he could to discourage them. He would point out the enemy's strength, the difficulty of defending against them, and the inevitable capture of the city. He didn't use a gun in his attack.

It wasn't necessary. ***His weapon was the power of discouragement.***

Satan attempts to do the same thing to us!

We are working on the negative effects of rejection that are listed in Deuteronomy 1:26-33. ***The next listed destructive effect of rejection is susceptibility to negative emotions.*** There are two negative emotions listed in this passage of Scripture: discouragement and fear. Discouragement is captured in

> Deuteronomy 1:28 (NASB), "²⁸ Where can we go up? Our brethren have made our hearts melt, saying, 'The people are bigger and taller than we; the cities are large and fortified to heaven. And besides, we saw the sons of the Anakim there.'"

The phrase "made our hearts melt" is another way of talking about discouragement. The KJV uses the words,

> "...our brethren have **discouraged** our heart..."

You may **not** think of discouragement as a feeling, because discouragement is a state. *However, discouragement is a state that has to do with depressed feelings. Discouragement is actually disheartenment, which is the loss of spirit or morale.* The word "spirit," in this context "is the feeling, quality or disposition characterizing something."[12] "Morale" is "the mental and emotional condition of an individual or group."[13] *Therefore, we should be able to see that discouragement is connected to a state of depressed or negative emotions.*

The second negative emotion is in

Deuteronomy 1:29 (NASB), "[29] Then I said to you, 'Do not be shocked, nor fear them.'"

*The second negative emotion listed is fear. Fear is a strong, unpleasant emotion that arises in anticipation of danger.* The word "shock" is a Hebrew word that means "to cause to tremble" (*NASB Greek & Hebrew Dictionary*).

---

[12] Merriam-Webster's Collegiate Dictionary.
[13] Merriam-Webster's Collegiate Dictionary.

*Therefore, shock or trembling is the physical manifestation of fear.*

*Notice that their fear flowed out of their discouragement. Discouragement and fear kept them from trusting God and going up to take the Promised Land in obedience to God.* Fear and faith in God are mutually exclusive, i.e. they cannot exist at the same time in the same space. If you fear anything other than God, you cannot have faith in God. If you have faith in God, you cannot fear anything else. *This is because you have faith in whatever you fear.* Therefore, you cannot have faith in something else and God at the same time. The Israelites feared their enemies. Therefore, they actually had faith that their enemies would beat them. Consequently, they didn't have faith that God could give them victory over their enemies.

*In addition, fear is intimately related to slavery.* Because the Israelites had been enslaved, there was a residue of fear remaining in their lives. Satan used that fear to keep them enslaved, in their own minds, and to keep them from entering the Promised Land. *Obviously, fear is a legitimate response to real danger, but it can also*

**be a <u>reactive</u> response to <u>perceived</u> danger.** Satan used the perceived danger of their enemies to keep their minds enslaved, which kept them from moving forward. In this case, their fear was nothing more than the acronym

**F***alse*
**E***vidences*
**A***ppearing*
**R***eal*

*There is one emotion listed in the text that I have <u>not</u> mentioned. It is the emotion of shame.* I believe shame also had a great deal to do with the Israelites' failure to take the Promised Land. Why? **Because, shame is a major byproduct of rejection.** There is **legitimate**, healthy, or deserved shame, which is guilt about **not** living up to an attainable standard. However, there is also an **illegitimate**, unhealthy, undeserved shame, which is a deep, negative feeling about self-image and worth, based upon standards that are imposed upon us by other people. *I believe the Israelites' labored with illegitimate shame, which resulted from their slavery, down in Egypt.*

I see, in our community, a great deal of illegitimate shame *miring* us in *mediocrity*. In our community, illegitimate shame stems from the secular culture, graceless churches, and non-accepting parents.

Before we make application of the truths we are learning concerning this destructive effective of rejection, we need to review our definition of a stronghold.

Edgardo Silvoso of Harvest Evangelism gives this definition of a stronghold:

"a stronghold is a mindset impregnated with hopelessness that causes the believer to accept as unchangeable something that he/she knows is contrary to the will of God."[1]

[1] Edgardo Silvoso, taken from a memorandum to supporters and friends on "Plan Resistencia," September 15, 1990: p. 3.

Now, we are ready for the application of these truths.

The definition of a stronghold can be interchanged with the definition for discouragement. Discouragement is a mindset impregnated with hopelessness that causes the believer to accept as unchangeable something that he/she knows is contrary to the will of God. *I see so many discouraged believers, and it saddens me!*

- We are discouraged about life!
- We are discouraged about our marriages!
- We are discouraged about our singleness!
- We are discouraged about our children!
- We are discouraged about our jobs!
- We are discouraged about our finances!
- We are discouraged about our friendships!
- We are discouraged about our suffering!
- Etc., etc., etc.

Consequently, discouragement leads to fear of the thing that we are discouraged about and we fear that the thing that we are discouraged about will never change.

As I thought about how to make application of this ravage of rejection, I believe the Lord impressed upon me to use the area of health through proper eating habits. Very few churches or preachers preach about this subject, yet I believe it is important.

Let me begin by saying that God is concerned about how we treat our bodies. Our bodies are the temples or dwelling places of our spirits, which are the dwelling places of the Holy Spirit. Satan is using unhealthy and addictive eating habits against us to destroy our victory and ultimately our lives.

Before we go any further, I want to state that I am **not** just talking to people who are overweight or "substantial." Some people are substantial, because of medical problems and medication. ***I am not as concerned about our weight as I am about our health and how our eating habits affect our health.*** It doesn't seem to dawn on modern people, but slim people can also have very unhealthy and addictive eating habits. Nevertheless, eating habits and a sedentary lifestyle have contributed to many Americans being overweight and malnourished. When I talk about being overweight, I am not talking about being a few pounds over the skimpy weight tables that do not represent different ethnicities. I am talking about being substantially above the weights listed on the weight tables. This has a direct relationship to the fat and sugar in the average American's diet—as well as some compulsive eating habits.

*I don't believe that everybody should be model thin; nor do I believe that everybody should be obese.* I believe that God has created us to arrive at an ideal, personal body weight, which corresponds to our body type—when we eat in a healthy manner. This ideal, personal body weight will be different from person-to-person and will fluctuate with the seasons of life. Our ideal body weight will **not** be the same at 21 years old as it will be at 51 years old.

In addition, I don't believe that you must diet to reach this ideal body weight. We will reach our ideal body weight by eating healthily, exercising, getting the proper amount of sleep, etc.

Mary Louise Bringle, author of the magazine article "Confessions of A Glutton" and "lifelong compulsive eater and dieter, calls for a theological response to this *wide-scale predicament*. (About 10-15% of the female students on college campuses are involved in binging and purging.)"[14] She

---

[14] Mary Louise Bringle, "Confessions of A Glutton," Christian Century, Oct 25, 1989, pp. 955-958.

goes on to say "compulsive dieting doesn't work— it is like trying to earn salvation. Diets don't work for both physiological and psychological/spiritual reasons."[15] **One of the interesting things that she states is that "the sin of gluttony is not against temperance but against trust, and the remedy lies in following the path of grace"**[16] (*bold type added*). Did you get that? We aren't gluttons simply because of a lack of self-control, but because we are not trusting God in some area of our lives. *With that lack of trust comes anxiety and fear, and we eat to anesthetize this pain!*

Jean Seligmann wrote in a Newsweek article back in 1992, "At any given time close to 50% of all American women and teenage girls are on a diet, *but the majority of them would not be medically classified as overweight*. ...Millions are driven to try to lose weight by fashion magazines, the fitness craze, and the dieting industry (a $33-billion-a-year business in the United

---

[15] Mary Louise Bringle, "Confessions of A Glutton," Christian Century, Oct 25, 1989, pp. 955-958.

[16] Mary Louise Bringle, "Confessions of A Glutton," Christian Century, Oct 25, 1989, pp. 955-958.

States)."[17] She goes on to report that researchers at a National Institutes of Health conference said that "yo-yo dieting probably ups the risk of heart disease more than being consistently overweight, and ninety percent of dieters regain the weight they lose soon after they stop dieting."[18]

*Therefore, I am __not__ advocating dieting, but Spirit-guided, healthy eating.*

*I believe that our eating habits are killing us!* I believe the high intake of sugar, meat, saturated fat, and processed foods are killing us. This kind of food is hard to digest, has little nutritional value, turns into fat, makes us sluggish, changes our emotional moods, affects our health, etc., etc., etc. Moreover, nobody wants to talk about it! It seems that we feel, "I am saved, so it's my business if I dig my grave with my fork! Is that so wrong?" Yes, it is wrong! Why? *Because, we are using food to medicate the pain of our rejection. We are turning to food when we are in pain. In short, food has become our god!*

---

[17] Jean Seligmann, "Let Them Eat Cake," Newsweek, Aug 1, 1992, pp. ages 57-58.

[18] Jean Seligmann, "Let Them Eat Cake," Newsweek, Aug 1, 1992, pp. ages 57-58.

This kind of teaching and thinking is so counter-culture that I feel the need to come at this again. Let's try this one more time. When you don't eat right, you don't feel good. When you don't feel good, often you don't have the motivation or energy to do the things that you ought to do. When you don't have the motivation or energy to do the things that you ought to do, it is much more difficult to live a victorious Christian life!

Then, Satan uses fear to keep us there. We fear the pain of trying to eat right. We fear the pain of trying to eat right and failing. Satan convinces us that we are better off where we are, rather than trying to free ourselves from his clutches. Through *False Evidences Appearing Real*, He keeps us trapped.

Well, there is certainly **no** simplistic answer to this problem. One answer is to attack the addiction and get it under control. Another answer is to deal with the rejection, which is the source of the discouragement and other ravages that are fueling the addiction. *But, in this book, we are working on praise!*

We have been discussing the fact that praise is a means of taking back territory from the enemy.

***One way to take back territory from the enemy is to get encouraged, rather than discouraged.*** Well, one way to get encouraged is to praise God.

When we eat, the brain releases special hormones called endorphins, into the brain's pathways. These endorphins cause the sensation of pleasure. ***Therefore, we eat to drown the pain of rejection with pleasure. The problem is that although God wants us to enjoy food, He doesn't want us to use food addictively to avoid dealing with pain in life.***

***Scientists are beginning to find out that when we praise God, the brain also releases endorphins.*** Therefore, we can begin to combat our discouragement by praising God. When we praise God, our brain releases endorphins and we experience pleasure. ***<u>Consequently, it's tough to stay discouraged when we are experiencing the pleasure of praising God</u>***.

Now, praise is **not** magic. Genuine praise is **not** guaranteed by any words, actions, or rituals. ***Genuine praise entails words and actions that flow from the heart.*** There are things about praise that we can influence and then there are things that we cannot influence and must come through the power of the Holy Spirit.

Okay, let's add another Bible verse to our glossary of verses on praise.

> Isaiah 30:31-32 (NASB), "³¹ For at the voice of the LORD Assyria will be terrified, When He strikes with the rod. ³² And every blow of the rod of punishment, Which the Lord will lay on him, Will be with the music of tambourines and lyres; And in battles, brandishing weapons, He will fight them."

**The satanic stronghold of rejection and the destructive effect of unhealthy eating habits are our enemies.** Therefore, they are also God's enemies. We know that when we praise God, He will arouse Himself and fight for us. **However, did you know that God fights His enemies with music?** Isaiah says that every blow that God lays on his enemies will be with music, i.e. with the music of tambourines and lyres. A lyre is a string instrument. **So, music is one way that we can fight our enemies.**

Once again, music, like praise releases endorphins into the brain. Therefore, when we praise God, in music, we can fight the enemies of discouragement and fear.

This goes beyond what happens at church. Get some music that puts you in a mood to praise and worship and use it in your car, in your study, in your bedroom, etc. Then, watch God fight your enemies for you!

# Chapter 9

# Rejection Deafens Us to God's Prophecy

## Emotions Can't Always Be Trusted

Emotions sometimes have a way of distorting our perception of reality. It's a bit like shining a flashlight on a sundial in the dark. By repositioning the flashlight you can make the sundial register any hour of the day you choose. This method will give you the desired reading, but it's hardly accurate.

It's like that when we allow our emotions to "shed light" on our circumstances. By manipulating the angle, we can get them to tell us almost anything we want to hear. Emotions can sometimes blind us to reality!

[*First Things First* by Stephen Covey, Roger Merrill, and Rebecca Merrill. Simon and Schuster, 1994.]

Likewise, emotions can also deafen us to the voice of God.

We are covering the destructive effects of rejection that are found in Deuteronomy 1:26-33. Remember that in this passage of Scripture, we do not see rejection proper, but the negative impact and destructive results of rejection. The Children of Israel were horribly rejected through the satanic device of slavery, down in Egypt, but their slavery entailed more than natural bondage. Their slavery entailed a spiritual bondage that was wrapped up with the idol gods and demons of the Egyptian religion. Even though God had gotten the Children of Israel out of slavery, He was still working to get slavery out of the Children of Israel. The past is often like the stenciled letters on my rearview mirror: "OBJECTS IN MIRROR ARE CLOSER THAN THEY APPEAR." What we often consider to be the past is very much a part of the present!

***The next listed destructive effect of rejection is the inability to hear God's words of***

***prophecy.*** Rejection deafened the Israelites to God's prophecy for them. God's prophecy for Israel is intimated in

> Deuteronomy 1:30 (NASB), "³⁰ The LORD your God who goes before you will Himself fight on your behalf, just as He did for you in Egypt before your eyes."

The words of this prophecy should have encouraged the Israelites, but they didn't! How do we know this? Because the Bible states that, "For all of this, they did not trust the LORD their God!"

"So, what happened?" Well, something was causing deafness to the God's Word. What was it? It seems obvious to me! In the last chapter, it was discouragement and fear that flowed from the stronghold of rejection. If you doubt my exposition and interpretation of this Scripture, Moses pointed out the root of this present discouragement in an earlier situation.

When the Children of Israel were still in bondage, down in Egypt, God spoke to Moses about delivering them from Egypt. However, God didn't stop there; He also spoke to Moses about the prophecy that He had given to Abraham. In the sixth (6ᵗʰ) chapter of Exodus, God told Moses

Exodus 6:5-9 (NASB), "⁵ Furthermore I have heard the groaning of the sons of Israel, because the Egyptians are holding them in bondage, and I have remembered My covenant. ⁶ Say, therefore, to the sons of Israel, 'I am the LORD, and I will bring you out from under the burdens of the Egyptians, and I will deliver you from their bondage. I will also redeem you with an outstretched arm and with great judgments. ⁷ Then I will take you for My people, and I will be your God; and you shall know that I am the Lord your God, who brought you out from under the burdens of the Egyptians. ⁸ I will bring you to the land which I swore to give to Abraham, Isaac, and Jacob, and I will give it to you *for* a possession; I am the LORD.' ⁹ So Moses spoke thus to the sons of Israel, but they did not listen to Moses on account of *their* despondency and cruel bondage."

These words capture several prophecies that directly relate to Israel's destiny. These words of prophecy should have brought great encouragement to the Israelites, but despondency and cruel bondage deafened them.

The word "despondency" literally means shortness of spirit. In the last chapter, one of the definitions of discouragement was loss of spirit or morale. Therefore, Moses is really talking about discouragement. Discouragement kept the Israelites from hearing the Word of God. ***Discouragement deafened the Israelites to God's prophecy!***

Now, please don't forget that we are **not** discussing the emotional/psychological impact of rejection, but the destructive effects of the satanic stronghold of rejection. ***We must understand that some deafness comes from physical causes, and some deafness is satanic.*** Remember what is recorded in

Mark 9:25 (NASB), "²⁵ When Jesus saw that a crowd was rapidly gathering, He

rebuked the unclean spirit, saying to it,
'You deaf and mute spirit, I command
you, come out of him and do not enter
him again.'"

**A demon can cause physical deafness,
but a demon can also cause spiritual deafness.** In fact, in the parable of "The Sower and
The Seed," in Matthew 13, we see four classes of
hearers. The seed obviously represents the Word
of God  There was

- Seed that fell by the roadside,
- Seed that fell on rocky places,
- Seed that fell among the thorns, and
- Seed that fell on good ground.

**Please note that birds ate up the seed that
fell by the roadside, and birds are often typ-
ical of demons.** That relationship is seen in
Revelation 18:2, where the terms "demons" and
"birds" are used synonymously. Consequently, in
the parable of "The Sower and The Seed," demons
ate up the seed of the Word of God, so that some
hearers couldn't hear it. Therefore, their hearing
of the Word of God was **supernaturally** blocked.

Likewise, in Deuteronomy 1, demons affected deafness to God's prophetic Word!

Our application of this material is wrapped up with satanic strongholds. Edgardo Silvoso of Harvest Evangelism gives this definition of a stronghold:

"a stronghold is a mindset impregnated with hopelessness that causes the believer to accept as unchangeable something that he/she knows is contrary to the will of God."[1]

[1] Edgardo Silvoso, taken from a memorandum to supporters and friends on "Plan Resistencia," September 15, 1990: p. 3.

We have come to a major reason why many of us can come to church, listen to powerful, Spirit-filled preaching, and never seem affected by it. The Word of God does **not** affect us, because we **cannot** hear it. The positive words of God's prophecy do **not** encourage us, because we are deaf to them. The ruling of negative emotions in our lives, particularly the **negative** emotions of discouragement, fear, and rejection, block us from hearing the **positive** prophecy of God's Word.

Let me say that again. We are sitting there; the Word is going forth; we seem to be listening; we may even be saying "Amen!" but a demonic deafness is dominating us.

Think of a positive biblical prophecy like the words of Jesus, the Christ, in

> John 10:10 (NASB), "[10] The thief comes only to steal and kill and destroy; I came that they may have life, and have *it* abundantly."

Jesus, the Christ, the Good Shepherd, the Great Shepherd, and the Chief Shepherd, states that He came to the earth that the sheep, i.e. everyone who believes in Him, i.e. us, might have life, and might have it abundantly. Jesus came to earth that we might have abundant life! These words should greatly encourage us. **It should be hard to be discouraged, fearful, and rejected, when we know that Jesus is bent on giving us abundant, overflowing, victorious life.**

So, why don't these and similar biblical words, encourage us and lift us above anything that Satan can throw at us? *Because we can't hear them!* They are **not** *living words* for our present situation, but *dead writings* of theological doctrine, which have little relationship to where we are. The positive prophecies of the Word of God can't do their full work in our lives, when we can't hear them. *I wonder how much of the Word of God simply reverberates in the auditoriums of churches across America without ever being heard?*

Now keep in mind that negative emotions that flow from the *satanic stronghold* of rejection effect our deafness to the prophecy of God's Word. Satan, the hellish spirit, and his evil horde are causing our deafness to the positive prophecies of God's Word.

- How many times have you sat in in church and experienced an unexplainable interference as you tried to hear the preaching of the Word of God?
- How many times have you sat in church and experienced an unexplainable interference as you tried to sing the songs of Zion?

- How many of those times have you been discouraged or disheartened?
- How many times have you thought that the interference was simply natural?

*I have written this book to let you know that the interference is often supernatural.* Satan uses discouragement as a spiritual earplug to keep us from hearing the positive, uplifting, encouraging Words of God!

*Now I can hear some of you thinking, "Since Satan uses the negative emotions of discouragement to block the Word of God, we should ignore these negative emotions. Right?"* "Wrong!" *Emotions have been given to us to alert us to the fact that something is wrong.* Negative emotions should alert us to the fact that something is wrong, that something or someone else is on the throne of our lives, that we are trusting something or someone other than Jehovah God, that our problems have become magnified and larger than God.

*Therefore, even though we should not allow these negative emotions to dictate our lives, we should not ignore them.* I view emotions as

141

indicators on the dashboard of life. On the dashboard in your car is an oil indicator. Often, it is a light. The light comes on when your engine oil is low. The light alerts you to the fact that something is wrong with your oil. ***Now, how you read and respond to that indicator depends upon your mental and emotional health.***

- Some people respond properly and fix the problem by setting an appointment to get the car into the shop for maintenance, as soon as possible.

- A respectable number of people simply ignore the indicator and wait until the engine is damaged.

- Some go under the dashboard and disconnect the indicator so that the light will no longer bother them.

- There are probably a few people who quit driving immediately.

Some overreact to the indicator and won't even drive the car in for maintenance.

This is the response of many people to emotions.

- Some people respond properly and address the problem or go in to the Manufacturer for maintenance.

*God made us and He can fix us. He doesn't need to fix the emotion. He will fix whatever that emotion points to!*

- Some people simply ignore their negative emotions and wait until there is an emotional breakdown.

Sanctified denial will **not** solve the problem of negative emotions.

- Some people go under the dashboard of their souls and completely disassociate from their emotions, so that they will **no** longer bother them. And,
- Some people simply give up on life.

These people overreact to negative emotions.

Although this isn't directly stated in the text we are studying, if discouragement is **not** cured it can lead to hardness of heart, and hardness of heart leads beyond deafness to rebellion. Remember the admonition of the writer of the Hebrews in

Hebrews 3:7-11 (NASB), "⁷ Therefore, just as the Holy Spirit says, 'TODAY IF YOU HEAR HIS VOICE, ⁸ DO NOT HARDEN YOUR HEARTS AS WHEN THEY PROVOKED ME, AS IN THE DAY OF TRIAL IN THE WILDERNESS, ⁹ WHERE YOUR FATHERS TRIED ME BY TESTING ME, AND SAW MY WORKS FOR FORTY YEARS. ¹⁰ THEREFORE I WAS ANGRY WITH THIS GENERATION, AND SAID, "THEY ALWAYS GO ASTRAY IN THEIR HEART, AND THEY DID NOT KNOW MY WAYS"; ¹¹ AS I SWORE IN MY WRATH, "THEY SHALL NOT ENTER MY REST.""'

The writer of the Hebrews is talking about what happened to the Israelites in the wilderness. When they were camped before the Promised Land, the first time, they were discouraged and that discouragement caused them to harden their hearts and refuse to go up and take the Promised Land.

So, how do we destroy the discouragement, fear, and rejection that Satan is using to deafen us to God's prophecy?

We are working on the statement "Praise is a means of taking back territory from the enemy!"

Let's add another Bible verse to our glossary of verses on praise.

> Psalm 9:1-3 (NASB), "¹ I will give thanks to the LORD with all my heart; I will tell of all Your wonders. ² I will be glad and exult in You; I will sing praise to Your name, O Most High. ³ When my enemies turn back, They stumble and perish before You."

- David pledges to give thanks to Jehovah God will all his heart.
- David pledges to testify about all the wonders of Jehovah God.
- David pledges to be glad and greatly rejoice in God.
- David pledges to sing praise to God's name.

***Now, notice the next phrase!*** It begins with the adverb "when." The next thing that we know, David's enemies are turning back. Not only are they turning back, but they are stumbling and perishing before Jehovah God.

Can't this be applied to us?

- When we give thanks to God with all our hearts;

This changes our hearts. It strengthens our hearts, while Satan is trying to discourage our hearts. Then,

- When we testify about all the wonders of God;
- When we are glad and greatly rejoice in God;
- When we sing praise to God's name;

Suddenly, before we know it, the enemies of our soul, discouragement, fear, and rejection are turning back before us; they are stumbling and perishing before Jehovah God.

With our enemies decimated, our ears are miraculously opened to hear God's prophecy concerning our destiny, and encouragement reigns in our lives.

Praise God now and watch your enemies turn back, stumble, and perish!

Praise God now and notice your ears opening up to God's words about your destiny!

# Chapter 10

# Rejection Blinds Us to God's Past Blessings

## Hourly Blessings

Henry Ward Beecher used to say: "If one should give me a dish of sand, and tell me that there were particles of iron in it, I might look for them with my eyes and search for them with my clumsy fingers, and be unable to detect them, but let me take a magnet and sweep through it, and how it would draw to itself the most invisible particles by the mere power of attraction! The unthankful heart, like my finger in the sand, discovers **no** mercies. But let the thankful heart sweep through the day, and as the magnet finds the iron, so my heart will find in every hour some heavenly blessings." [Servant, Nov 1994. Page 15.]

Rejection demagnetizes the heart, so that it loses its ability to find blessings for which to thank God.

The next listed effect of rejection is **blindness to God's past blessings**. This destructive effect is seen in the words of

> Deuteronomy 1:30-31 (NASB-U), "The LORD your God who goes before you will Himself fight on your behalf, just as He did for you in Egypt before your eyes, [31] and in the wilderness where you saw how the LORD your God carried you, just as a man carries his son, in all the way which you have walked until you came to this place."

Moses reminds the Israelites of the past blessings of the LORD:

1. He fought for them in Egypt, **before their eyes**.
2. He also fought for them in the wilderness.
3. They **saw** how the LORD carried them.

Moses doesn't stop there, but describes the way in which Jehovah God carried them. God carried them as a man carries his son. He didn't just carry them part of the way, but in all the way which they walked, until they reached the present place—i.e. camped in front of the Promised Land.

God fought for them in Egypt; He fought for them in the wilderness; and He carried them in the wilderness! However, there is something very interesting about this short passage of Scripture. Moses is trying to point something out to the Israelites. *He points out two times that the Children of Israel saw what God did.* Now, if they saw how God had blessed them in the past, why weren't they willing to go up and take the Promised Land? Answer: because even though they had *physically seen* the blessings of God, they were *spiritually blinded* to God's past blessings when it came time to believe, act, and obey. Rejection blinded the Israelites to the spiritual implications of God's past blessings, so that those blessings didn't have the effect that they were supposed to have. The despondency of rejection **not** only deafened them to God's words of prophecy; it blinded them to the spiritual blessings of God's acts.

Therefore, they never *spiritually* saw the blessings of God!

Remember, we are viewing these ravages of rejection through the prism of strongholds. Edgardo Silvoso of Harvest Evangelism gives this definition of a stronghold:

> "a stronghold is a mindset impregnated with hopelessness that causes the believer to accept as unchangeable something that he/she knows is contrary to the will of God."[1]
>
> ---
> [1]  Edgardo Silvoso, taken from a memorandum to supporters and friends on "Plan Resistencia," September 15, 1990: p. 3.

*I see strongholds in our lives with respect to God's past blessings.* I believe that we acknowledge the blessings when they occur and we may

even verbally praise and thank Him for His blessings, but we don't **spiritually** see those blessings
for what they are. **The stronghold of rejection
blinds us to the true nature of the blessings
of God.** Therefore, when we face a challenge, the
blessings aren't recalled because our minds are
impregnated with hopelessness. This hopelessness acts as a blinder that keeps us from remembering God's past blessings in a way that would
encourage us to go up and possess the Promised
Land. **We accept as unchangeable our hopeless conditions, even though we know that
this is contrary to the will of God.**

For example:

- Often, God will bless us to overcome an
  obstacle on our jobs, but we can't **seem**
  to see that, when we face another obstacle
  on our jobs.

- Sometimes God will bless us with specific provisions during tough times, but we
  can't **seem** to see that as we approach various problems.

- Sometimes God gives us a specific blessing
  with respect to a difficult friendship or relationship, but we don't **seem** to be able to

see that when it comes to relationships in our home.

- Often God blesses us to handle our finances wisely enough to make some progress, but we can't **seem** to see those blessings when He encourages us to get out of debt.

- God often blesses us to begin to get our eating habits under control, but we can't *seem* to remember that when a Krispy Kreme doughnut comes our way.

- God often blesses us to begin to grow, but we can't see those blessings when we face a challenge to live victorious lives.

The blessings of the LORD seem short-lived and we don't seem to remember them when we face our next challenge or trial. Why? The stronghold of rejection, i.e. the mindset of hopelessness blinds us to the spiritual implication of God's past blessings.

The implications are multitudinous, but let me give you just one: *If God took care of us in the past and He is taking care of us in the present, surely He will take care of us in the future.* The songwriter put it this way:

He didn't bring us this far to leave us.
He didn't teach us to swim to let us drown.
He didn't build a home in us to move away, and
He didn't lift us up to let us down!

"How do we remove the obstacles that are blinding us to God's past blessings?"

*"Praise is a means of taking back territory from the devil!"* Moreover, the kind of praise that the Israelites should have given for past blessings was thanksgiving! In a message series entitled "Close Encounters of the God kind," I developed the following words: "The remembrance of God's past blessings or the remembrance of the redemptive past should facilitate or precipitate a genuine response of worship." *In other words, remembering what God has already done should bring about a genuine response of worship, and that response should primarily be thanksgiving.*

Therefore, whether we understand it or not, we can also say

"**Thanksgiving** is a means of taking back territory from the devil!"

I need to expand this, because most of us don't think of thanksgiving as praise, but technically it is. ***Thanksgiving is one kind of praise.*** The writer of the Hebrews said in

> Hebrews 13:15-16 (NASB), "[15] Through Him then, let us continually offer up a sacrifice of praise to God, that is, the fruit of lips that give thanks to His name. [16] And do not neglect doing good and sharing, for with such sacrifices God is pleased."

***There are three sacrifices of praise that are listed in this tremendous verse, but I only want to deal with one: the fruit of lips that give thanks to His name.*** Consequently, here we have a direct statement that one of the sacrifices of praise is thanksgiving.

So, thanksgiving is the public acknowledgement of God's goodness. Thanksgiving is a recounting of God's past blessings! ***Moreover, one who***

*constantly recounts God's past blessings is*
*going to be positively changed!*

- Thanksgiving changes our attitude from negative to positive.
- Thanksgiving also changes our perception of our circumstances.
- Thanksgiving changes us.

In that "Close Encounter" message series, we also learned that "a response of genuine worship or celebration...changes people forever; causing them to move and grow by over-recording the intuitive tapes of their core belief."

The Israelites' core belief was filled with rejection. However, the praise response of thanksgiving would change them forever, by over-recording the intuitive tapes (or mp3's) of their core belief!

The intuitive tapes of their core belief, which automatically run messages of rejection, would be over-recorded with acceptance and courage if they persisted in thanksgiving! This is specifically stated in

Deuteronomy 7:17-18 (NASB), "¹⁷ If you should say in your heart, 'These

155

nations are greater than I; how can I dispossess them?' [18] you shall not be afraid of them; you shall well remember what the LORD your God did to Pharaoh and to all Egypt."

God is saying, "When you remember how I delivered you, it will bring about thanksgiving and praise that will precipitate courage, and you will go up and take the Promised Land."

This is just as applicable to us! The remembrance of the redemptive past should facilitate or precipitate a genuine response of worship. The specific response ought to be **the praise of thanksgiving**. **The praise of thanksgiving** changes us forever, causing us to move and grow by over-recording our intuitive tapes. Hope**less**ness is over-recorded by Hope**ful**ness!

Therefore, the tradition of **good** African-American preaching highlights the redemptive past. We know that at some time in almost every sermon, we are going to look back and

- Remember where God has brought us from,

"He brought me from a mighty long way!"

- Remember what He delivered us from,

"He saved my soul from sin and shame!"

- Remember how He brought us out,

"He brought me out of abuse, drugs, alcohol, and other impacts of slavery!"

- Remember how He made a way out of no way,
- Remember how He redeemed us from the slave market of sin or some condition of bondage.

Therefore, the preacher is going to ask you:
- Has God **saved** anybody in here?
- Has God **delivered** anybody in here?
- Has God **kept** anybody in here?

Then, let the redeemed of the Lord say so! Somebody say, "Yes!" Somebody say, "Thank you Jesus!" Somebody say, "Hallelujah!" If you have never been delivered from some form of bondage, you don't know what we are talking about!

This remembrance of a redemptive past is "a genuine response of worship" that transforms the events immediately experienced or changes the person forever. ***From this "genuine response of worship," people receive the courage to do or face what they could <u>not</u> do or face just a few moments before.***

- Frightened civil rights workers were transformed into dog-fighting, fire-hose fighting missionaries.
- Abused wives are changed into courageous women, who confront their abusers.
- Deadbeat dads are changed into fathers of integrity.
- Children who are harassed on the playgrounds of America are changed into flaming preachers of Christ.
- Hopeless, retiring saints are changed into hopeful Lions of righteousness, who are as harmless as doves.

The problem that I have with some African-American preaching is that the preachers often start asking these questions and exhorting these responses before the text has been explored or they do this completely disjointed from the text. *They are adding foreign gravy to the meat. A good meat makes its own gravy!*

*Not only does thanksgiving change us and render us ready to do the will of God, it also arouses God to fight on our behalf, defeat our enemies, rescue us, and give us back territory that rightfully belongs to us.* Let me give you one Scripture and one example. The Scripture is found in

> Psalm 50:14-15 (NASB), "[14] Offer to God a sacrifice of thanksgiving And pay your vows to the Most High; [15] Call upon Me in the day of trouble; I shall rescue you, and you will honor Me."

Asaph, the Levitical musician appointed by David, is giving us the Words of God. Is God prescribing a formula for activating His help? He says, in effect, "Offer a sacrifice of thanksgiving to Me and pay your worship vows to me. Then call upon Me in the day of your trouble and I will rescue you." *It appears that a sacrifice of thanksgiving moves God to rescue us, when we call upon Him.*

Therefore, let's cultivate an attitude of gratitude; let's become thankful and work at thanksgiving; let's give God the sacrifice of thanksgiving or praise, continually; let's constantly rehearse God's past blessings. ***Then, let us watch God rescue us from the stronghold of rejection!***

Let's consider an example of how this process works.

In Israel's history, there was a time when the sons of Moab and the sons of Ammon together with some of the Meunites, came to make war against King Jehoshaphat, king of Judah (*2 Chron. 20*). Some of the people came and reported to Jehoshaphat that a great multitude was coming against him, and Jehoshaphat was afraid. Therefore, he turned his attention to seek the LORD and proclaimed a fast throughout all Judah.

So, all of Judah gathered together to seek the LORD. Jehoshaphat stood up in the assembly of the people and prayed a magnificent prayer of importunity or urgent need.

To make a long story short, when they got up the next day they prepared to meet their enemies. In preparation, Jehoshaphat, evidently, told Jahaziel, the chief musician, to gather his praise team. He told Jahaziel, "The praise team is going to lead us into battle today!" Now there is something that had never been tried before, but Jehoshaphat was putting His trust in God. Consequently, Jahaziel gathered up the members of the praise team and they went out in front of the army saying and singing,

> "Give thanks to the LORD, for His loving-kindness is everlasting."

Now, when they began singing, praising, and thanking God, God used praise against their enemies and they were routed! ***Praise God right now!***

Thanksgiving aroused God to fight on behalf of His people!

Years ago, I remember feeling tired and the Saints would sing:

> I give thanks unto the LORD for His goodness to me;
> Thanks unto the LORD for His goodness to me.
> His mercy endureth forever;
> I give thanks, I give thanks unto the LORD.

And, before you know it, God had lifted the heaviness of the enemy!

***Thanksgiving aroused God to fight on behalf of His people! Do you think that is applicable today?*** Is God the same God today, yesterday, and forever? Then I dare you to start thanking and praising God and see if He won't set ambushes against the stronghold of rejection.

I dare you to repeat these words out loud:

"Give thanks to the LORD, for His lovingkindness is everlasting."

"Give thanks to the LORD, for His lovingkindness is everlasting."

"Give thanks to the LORD, for His loving kindness is everlasting."

- Do you sense strongholds falling in your life?
- Do you feel bondages being broken in your life?
- Do you believe that enemies of your soul are being routes?

***Rejection blinds us to the spiritual implication of God's past blessings, but thanksgiving removes the blinders and arouses God to fight on our behalf!***

# Chapter 11

# Rejection Effects a Lack of Trust in God

## Taking God at His Word

A pastor tells about the first time he ever went skiing: "When I arrived at the ski resort, I decided to tackle one of the more advanced slopes. After all, I was an expert skier on the carpeted skiing machine in the sporting goods store.

Boy, did I receive a rude awakening! After tumbling down a large hill several times, the ski instructors finally escorted me to the 'bunny' hill, but I soon regained my confidence after going through the new skier's class.

While riding up the mountain on a chair lift, I saw something I could hardly believe. Small children—about 5 or 6 years old—were skiing effortlessly down a rather steep slope.

I asked the ski instructor, 'How long have those kids been taking lessons?'

'About a day,' he replied.

'How could they learn so fast when so many adults—like me—take so long just learning to get down the bunny hill?'

'Because they believe the words of the instructor and expect those words to work.'"

"This is the essence of releasing hope. To regain the ability to expect, dream, and envision, we must learn to trust the words of the Instructor. When we take God at His Word—with childlike trust— we will begin to see the fulfillment of our dreams." [Charisma, Mar 1994. Pages 46-47.]

As adults, we often have trouble trusting God, because of the ravages of rejection.

The next destructive effect of rejection is seen in

> Deuteronomy 1:32 (NASB), "³² But for all this, you did not trust the LORD your God."

The phrase "for all this" is literally "in this matter." The matter that Moses is talking about is the taking of the Promised Land. The Israelites did **not** trust God to fulfill His promise and give them the Promised Land. ***The Israelites did <u>not</u> rely upon God by putting their full weight down upon His promise.*** I liken this kind of trust to sitting in a chair.

- Biblical trust has nothing to do with the modern, Evangelical, Greek-influenced idea of believing in propositional statements about the chair.
- Biblical trust has nothing to do with understanding the engineering specifications of the chair.
- Biblical trust has nothing to do with believing that the chair can hold you.
- ***Biblical trust is <u>not</u> academic; it is practical and relational!***
- Biblical trust is sitting in the chair!

Now, as I studied this verse, I wondered why the NAS translators would translate the phrase we are looking at "for all this," when the notes say that it is literally "in this matter" and the KJV translates it "in this thing." Well, when I ran the computer reference on this verse, it took me to

> Numbers 14:11, "And the LORD said to Moses, 'How long will this people spurn Me? And how long will they not believe in Me, despite all the signs which I have performed in their midst?'"

This verse is additional commentary on this situation. They did **not** believe God despite all the signs which God had performed in their midst. The phrase "for all this" corresponds to the word "signs" in Numbers 14:11. *In the passage of Scripture before us, the phrase "for all this" refers to the fact that God fought for them in Egypt and carried them in the wilderness, as a man carries his son, all the way to their present encampment before the Promised Land.* Now, in the light of all of this, why didn't the Israelites trust in God? *Because, rejection effects a lack of trust in God!*

In our application of these truths, we have been looking at strongholds. Edgardo Silvoso of Harvest Evangelism gives this definition of a stronghold:

> "a stronghold is a mindset impregnated with hopelessness that causes the believer to accept as unchangeable something that he/she knows is contrary to the will of God."[1]

[1] Edgardo Silvoso, taken from a memorandum to supporters and friends on "Plan Resistencia," September 15, 1990: p. 3.

Now, there are some situations and times in life, when you must simply act! You must simply trust in God! As an older Nike ad campaign urged, "Just do it!" By the way, the word *Nike* is a Greek word which denotes victory. There are places in the Bible, where God exhorts His people to simply put their trust in Him. One of those places is where the sons of Moab, the sons of Ammon, and the Meunites gather to war against Jehoshaphat. The Bible says in

2 Chronicles 20:20 (NASB), "[20] They rose early in the morning and went out to the wilderness of Tekoa; and when they

went out, Jehoshaphat stood and said, 'Listen to me, O Judah and inhabitants of Jerusalem, put your trust in the LORD your God and you will be established. Put your trust in His prophets and succeed.'"

Another very familiar exhortation to trust God is in

Proverbs 3:5 (NASB), "⁵ Trust in the LORD with all your heart And do not lean on your own understanding."

*Therefore, at some point, we must prove God by exercising our trust in Him!* I have done this for every piece of property, every loan, and every building.

*Nevertheless, I want to point out that a lack of trust in God is not a simple thing.* Preaching and teaching, in our day, makes it seem like trust, or the lack thereof, is simple and straightforward. You either believe the propositions about God or you don't believe them. *Yet, I am maintaining that trust in God is neither simple nor academic.*

*Biblical trust does not occur in the intellect, but in the realm of the emotions.* It has much more to do with our intuitions than our minds. The opposite of faith is fear, and we know that fear is an emotion. Yet, it is very difficult for us, particularly in America, to understand that trust is more of an emotion or core value belief than an intellectual belief.

*Secondarily, when there is a predisposition to disbelief or distrust, no amount of proof can undo that predisposition. The Children of Israel had a predisposition to disbelieve or not trust God.* Some of the biblical things that I have taught never had a chance of being believed or trusted, because many people were closed before the teaching ever went forth.

So, how do we develop trust in God?

Trust in God is developed through an intimate relationship and fellowship with Him. However, how do we develop this kind of relationship and fellowship, when rejection is so powerful in our lives? I believe the answer is in a personal encounter with Jehovah God and one kind of personal encounter is through intake and illumination of the Word of God.

> Romans 10:17, "So faith comes from hearing, and hearing by the word of Christ."

When Paul uses the word "hearing," I don't believe he is excluding all other modes of receiving the Word of God. Remember that in the Mediterranean culture the average person did not have access to the Word of God and could not read. He is simply touching on the most common and one of the most powerful ways of receiving the Word of God, i.e. through preaching. It also goes without saying that Paul is **not** talking about some magical intake of the Word of God. He is talking about receiving the message of the Bible, and the illumination of the Holy Spirit that is necessary for the message to be effectively heard. ***Effective intake of the Word of God will produce faith or trust in God.*** The concept is the same as in the Old Testament. "New Testament 'faith' is trust. The word here is *pistis*. Kittle's *Theological Dictionary of The New Testament* Says,

"3. *pistis* has the sense of a. "confidence," "certainty," "trust," then b. "trustworthiness," and c. "guarantee" or "assurance" in the sense of a pledge or oath with the two nuances of "trustworthiness" and "proof."[19]

Well, we have been talking about the fact that ***praise is a means of taking back territory from the devil.*** By praising God, we are changing our perception and ultimately our conception of God. One of the major ways that we can do this is through thanksgiving. ***Now I am not talking about the attitude of thankfulness, but the action of thanksgiving.*** The attitude of thankfulness is obviously a prerequisite to the action of thanksgiving. Thanksgiving is a kind of worship and a form of praise. When we thank God, we worship Him by giving Him that which is due His name, but we also praise Him. Praise is the public proclamation of who God is or what He has done. Thanksgiving is praising God for the things that He has done.

---

[19] Kittel, Gerhard, and Friedrich, Gerhard, Editors, *The Theological Dictionary of the New Testament, Abridged in One Volume*, (Grand Rapids, Michigan: William B. Eerdmans Publishing Company) 1985.

The Bible says in

1 Thessalonians 5:18, "In everything give thanks; for this is God's will for you in Christ Jesus."

Ephesians 5:18-20, "And do not get drunk with wine, for that is dissipation, but be filled with the Spirit, speaking to one another in psalms and hymns and spiritual songs, singing and making melody with your heart to the Lord; ***always giving thanks for all things*** in the name of our Lord Jesus Christ to God, even the Father" (*bold italics added*).

***One way to take back territory from the devil and cultivate trust is to make up our minds to constantly give thanks to God for all things.*** Now, you should be asking, "But how can I do that when I really don't feel it?" Well, we can begin to feel it, when we have come to experience the fact that all things work together for good to those who love God and are called according to His purpose.

***I believe that we can begin to cultivate trust in God, by thanking God in advance for what we know He is going to do.*** Jesus taught in

> Mark 11:24, "Therefore I say to you, all things for which you pray and ask, believe that you have received them, and they shall be granted you."

If we believe that God has already granted our prayer requests, then isn't it logical to thank Him for them in advance?!

Not only should thank God in advance, but perhaps we should shout in advance. At the battle of Jericho, the Israelites were to remain silent for six days, as they circled the walls of Jericho. But on the seventh day they circled the walls seven times and the Bible says in

> Joshua 6:16 (NASB), "¹⁶ At the seventh time, when the priests blew the trumpets, Joshua said to the people, 'Shout! For the Lord has given you the city.'"

Trust in God was exhibited, when they shouted in reliance upon God's promise. Trust in God is exhibited, when we shout because we trust God's promise!

- Shout, right now, because God has given you the city of your inheritance and destiny.
- Shout, right now, because you trust God to free you from the satanic stronghold of rejection.
- Shout, right now, because you ***trust God*** to give you abundant, victorious, overcoming Christian life.

# Chapter 12

# Rejection Perverts Our Perception of God's Providence

W hen I worked at Babcock & Wilcox Co., in Barberton, Ohio, God sent Al Spivey across my path to help me get a solid start in the ministry. Al was a saved, White brother, from the GARBC (General Association of Regular Baptist Churches), who prophesied into my life and gave me solid biblical books to read. One of the books that he gave me was on the life of George Mueller. I would like to share a story that was instrumental in forming my fledgling faith!

## Breakfast from God

Things looked bleak for the children in George Mueller's orphanage at Ashley Downs in England. It was time for breakfast, and there was **no** food. A small girl whose father was a close friend of Mueller's was visiting in the home. Mueller took her hand and said, "Come and see what our Father will do." In the dining room, long tables were set with empty plates and empty mugs. Not only was there **no** food in the kitchen, but there was no money in the home's account. Mueller prayed, "Dear Father, we thank Thee for what Thou art going to give us to eat." Immediately, they heard a knock at the door. When they opened it, there stood the local baker. "Mr. Mueller," he said, "I couldn't sleep last night. Somehow, I felt you had no bread for breakfast, so I got up at 2 o'clock and baked fresh bread. Here it is." Mueller thanked him and gave praise to God. Soon, a second knock was heard. It was the milkman. His cart had broken down in front of the orphanage. He said he would like to give the children the milk so he could empty the cart and repair it.

Why could George Mueller pray with such confidence? ***Because, he had seen God take care of the children many times before.*** C. H. Spurgeon, the prince of preachers, once said, "It is not to be imagined that He who has helped us in six troubles will leave us in the seventh." ***Yet, sometimes our perception of God's divine providence is perverted!***

As we come to the end of this book, let's do a little review.

I have been covering the ravages or destructive effects of rejection that I discerned in Deuteronomy 1:26-33.

> Deuteronomy 1:26-33 (NASB), "²⁶ Yet you were not willing to go up, but rebelled against the command of the LORD your God; ²⁷ and you grumbled in your tents and said, 'Because the LORD hates us, He has brought us out of the land of Egypt to deliver us into the hand of the Amorites to destroy us. ²⁸ Where can we go up? Our brethren have made our hearts melt, saying, "The people are bigger and taller than

we; the cities are large and fortified to heaven. And besides, we saw the sons of the Anakim there.'" [29] Then I said to you, 'Do not be shocked, nor fear them. [30] The LORD your God who goes before you will Himself fight on your behalf, just as He did for you in Egypt before your eyes, [31] and in the wilderness where you saw how the LORD your God carried you, just as a man carries his son, in all the way which you have walked until you came to this place.' [32] But for all this, you did not trust the LORD your God, [33] who goes before you on *your* way, to seek out a place for you to encamp, in fire by night and cloud by day, to show you the way in which you should go."

The name "Deuteronomy" means the second giving of the Law. The Children of Israel are now camped in front of the Promised Land. They had been wandering through the wilderness for 40 years, while everyone 20 years old and older, who had **not** trusted God to take them into the

Promised Land the first time, were allowed to die as God stepped back from them. Moses, who is about to die, is now looking back over the past 40 years and talking to the Israelites about finally entering the Promised Land.

In this passage of Scripture, we do **not** see rejection proper, but the ***negative impact*** and ***destructive results*** of rejection. The Children of Israel were horribly rejected through the ***satanic device of slavery***, down in Egypt, but their slavery entailed more than natural bondage. ***Their slavery entailed a spiritual bondage that was wrapped up with the idol gods and demons of the Egyptian religion. Even though God had gotten the Children of Israel out of slavery, He was still working to get slavery out of the Children of Israel.*** The past is often like the stenciled letters on my rearview mirror: **"OBJECTS IN MIRROR ARE CLOSER THAN THEY APPEAR."** ***What we often consider to be the past is very much a part of the present!***

All right, the final listed effect of rejection was the Israelites' perverted perception of God's providence. This is seen in

Deuteronomy 1:32-33 (NASB), "[32] But
for all this, you did not trust the LORD
your God, [33] who goes before you on
*your* way, to seek out a place for you
to encamp, in fire by night and cloud
by day, to show you the way in which
you should go.

Before we go any further, what is divine providence? ***Divine providence is God's faithful
and effective care of everything in our lives
towards the outcome that He has chosen.***
Shirley Caesar sang a song that puts it in everyday
terms. Shirley sang "He's Working It Out!" God
has a destiny for His children and He is working
that destiny out through His faithful and effective care of everything in the lives of His children
towards that destiny. "He's working it out!" No
matter what is going on in your life, if you are
saved God is working it out!

God's divine providence, in the passage of
Scripture before us, is seen in the context of Him
going before the Israelites to seek out a place for
them to camp. The outcome that God had chosen
for the Children of Israel was the Promised Land.

*God was taking faithful and effective care of everything in the lives of the Israelites towards that outcome.* This divine care included a pillar of fire by night and pillar of cloud by day to show the Israelites the way that they should go. *Moreover, you know what? They made it!*

Think about it. Imagine what it would have been like to see those pillars of fire by night and cloud by day guiding and guarding you. *The two pillars of God's legs walking amid the camp!*

However, after God miraculously delivered the Children of Israel from Egypt, they ran into an impossible situation. They were trapped with the Red Sea in front of them, mountains to either side of them, and Pharaoh's army coming behind them. In this situation, the pillar moved from in front of them to behind them and separated them from Pharaoh's army. *The Bible says that both YHWH and the angel of God were in that cloud leading the children of Israel to the Promised Land.* Moreover, since the cloud and fire were the manifest presence of God, the Holy Spirit was also present in those manifestations. Therefore, YHWH, the pre-incarnate Christ and the Holy Spirit were in those manifestations.

Now, the cloud gave darkness and confusion to the Egyptians, but light and direction to the Israelites. The cloud separated them all night long, while God opened the Red Sea by the blast of His mighty nostrils. That had to be an awesome experience, but that was **not** all.

From that point forward, the pillar never left them, but went before them to lead them to the Promised Land. The Bible says in

> Exodus 13:21-22 (NASB), "²¹ The LORD was going before them in a pillar of cloud by day to lead them on the way, and in a pillar of fire by night to give them light, that they might travel by day and by night. ²² He did not take away the pillar of cloud by day, nor the pillar of fire by night, from before the people."

Now you would think that the Children of Israel would trust a God who demonstrated such providential care for them, yet God said, "But for all this you did **not** trust the LORD your God..."

- Why couldn't the Israelites trust God, in the light of His providence in bringing them up out of Egypt, the house of bondage?
- Why couldn't the Israelites trust God, in the light of His providential deliverance through the Red Sea on dry land?
- Why couldn't the Israelites trust God, in the light of God's providence in that pillar of fire by night and pillar of cloud by day?

*The Israelites couldn't trust God in the light of His providential care, because they couldn't accurately see God's providential care. The stronghold of rejection perverted their perception of God's providence.* They saw the providential workings of God, but they could **not** understand them or receive them for what they really were: *God's faithful and effective care of everything in their lives towards the outcome that He had chosen.*

Their perception of God's providence is stated in

Deuteronomy 1:27bc (NASB), "'Because the LORD hates us, He has brought us

out of the land of Egypt to deliver us into
the hand of the Amorites to destroy us."

Their perverted perception was that God had
delivered them from Egypt and led them by a
pillar of fire by night and a pillar of cloud by day,
so that He might deliver them into the hands of
their enemies to destroy them. ***This is so perverted and very sad.***

This perversion is **not** just physical, or even
psychological, but spiritual. ***There are some
things that can only be spiritually discerned.***
The stronghold of rejection spiritually perverted
their perception of God's providence.

For the last time, let's review Edgardo Silvoso's
definition of a stronghold.

> "A stronghold is a mindset impreg-
> nated with hopelessness that causes
> the believer to accept as unchangeable
> something that he/she knows is con-
> trary to the will of God."[20]

---

[20] Edgardo Silvoso, taken from a memorandum to supporters and
friends on "Plan Resistencia," September 15, 1990: p. 3.

Many of us, like the Children of Israel, have a perverted perception of God's providence in our lives. This perverted perception is the destructive effect of the stronghold of rejection. The stronghold of rejection has produced in us a mindset impregnated with hopelessness that perverts our perception of God's providence and causes us to accept as unchangeable an outcome and destiny that we know is contrary to God's will.

First, let's talk about this from a corporate perspective. Is it possible that the stronghold of rejection is perverting our perception concerning God's divine providence towards our church? You may be thinking, "What do you mean Bishop?" God has demonstrated His providential care on our behalf that we might know that He is our God and trust Him. Nevertheless, what have we made of

- God saving thousands of people.
- God giving us our first building after it was already sold.
- The Christian Missionary Alliance giving us a second mortgage larger than the first mortgage on our second building.

185

- God making various pieces of property available, when they seemed to be totally unavailable.
- God giving us the JC Penney's building for our prophesied price.
- God granting us a loan for our first construction project so early in our history.
- God granting us the grace to successfully complete several construction projects.
- God granting us a $3.3 million-dollar loan.
- God granting us $9 million dollars in loans.

Yet, the stronghold of rejection is impregnating some of our minds with hopelessness, and we can't see the divine providence of God. ***Some of us are satanically blocked from seeing the providential leading of the Lord in our midst.*** Let's move from a corporate level to a personal level. ***God blesses each one of us to let us know that we can trust Him to give us a destiny and an inheritance, but the stronghold of rejection impregnates our minds with hopelessness and perverts our perception concerning God's divine providence in our lives.*** It is God who watches over us every day and is orchestrating the faithful and effective care of **everything** towards the outcome of our destiny. His providence is seen in the fact that

- He leads us through the power of the Holy Spirit, by day and by night.
- He protects us from our enemies.
- He nourishes us with the water of the Holy Spirit and the manna of the Word of God.
- He keeps our feet from swelling, i.e. He sustains us physically.
- He keeps our shoes from wearing out, i.e. He sustains us materially.
- He opens doors that seem to be closed.
- He closes doors that are opened. And
- Anything that comes into our lives must be sifted through His providential care.

*God is working out everything in our lives that we might know Him and trust Him to give us a destiny!*

Yet, the stronghold of rejection causes us to be filled with hopelessness concerning our destiny and a perverted perception of God's divine providence in our lives. ***Have you ever seen God's providential pillar of fire in the dark*** *night of your soul and yet felt unable to trust God and walk after the light of that moving pillar?* I have! There are times when I have seen the light of God's providence leading me in a certain direction, but because of ravages of rejection, I wondered whether God was leading me to the Promised Land or over a cliff. Praise God that He has been gracious enough with me to give me another chance and enough power to follow Him in His next leading.

So, how do we overcome this perverted perception?

Of course, the answer is varied and complex, but let me give a few suggestions.

First, we need to deal with the stronghold of rejection, but that is the very long-term process that we have been discussing. So, let's go on to the next suggestion.

*One of the things that we want to do is activate and develop spiritual discernment, which is a function of the ministry of the Holy Spirit in our lives.* Amazingly, the necessary faculties for discerning God's destiny are **not cerebral**, but **spiritual**. Paul talked about this in

1 Corinthians 2:14 (NASB), "¹⁴ But a natural man does not accept the things of the Spirit of God, for they are foolishness to him; and he cannot understand them, because they are spiritually appraised."

*Therefore, to develop spiritual discernment, we must first be spiritual or filled with the Spirit.*

Ephesians 5:18-20 (NASB), "¹⁸ And do not get drunk with wine, for that is dissipation, but be filled with the Spirit, ¹⁹ speaking to one another in psalms and hymns and spiritual songs, singing and making melody with your heart to the Lord; ²⁰ always giving thanks for all things in the name of our Lord Jesus Christ to God, even the Father."

In the verse before us, we can see that being filled with the Spirit has something to do with singing and making melody with our hearts to the Lord. *Now, we are back to the healing thesis of*

189

*this series: praise is a means of taking back territory from the devil.* We can begin to take back perceptual territory from the devil, when we being to praise and worship God by singing and making melody with our hearts to the Lord. When we sing to God with all our hearts or wholeheartedly, i.e. with our spirits, with our souls (intellect, emotion, and will), and with our bodies, then we are praising God with all that is within us. *When we praise God with all that is within us, we are preparing our hearts and welcoming the Holy Spirit to fill us.*

So, from now on, let us sing wholeheartedly to the Lord! Let's put some "oomph" into it! When we do, the Spirit will fill us and we can rely upon His discernment.

*Being filled with the Spirit also has something to do with always giving thanks for all things to God, in the name of Christ Jesus.* Cultivating the action of thanksgiving for all things prepares our hearts and welcomes the Holy Spirit to fill us.

So, from now on, let's thank God for everything that comes into our lives. When we do, the Holy Spirit will fill us and we can rely upon His discernment to perceive the divine providence of God on our behalf. We will be able to see what the hymn writer saw, when he wrote

> Through many dangers, toils, and snares I have already come; His grace has brought me safe thus far and grace will lead me home.

This spiritual insight will build trust in God and we will go up and take the Promised Land of abundant, overcoming, victorious life!

However, I want to summarize all the Scriptures and teaching that we have touched on concerning praise with one resolve:

> Psalm 34:1, "I will bless the Lord at all times; His praise shall continually be in my mouth."

This resolve will lead us towards taking back territory from the devil and making the stronghold of rejection the stronghold of the Lord!

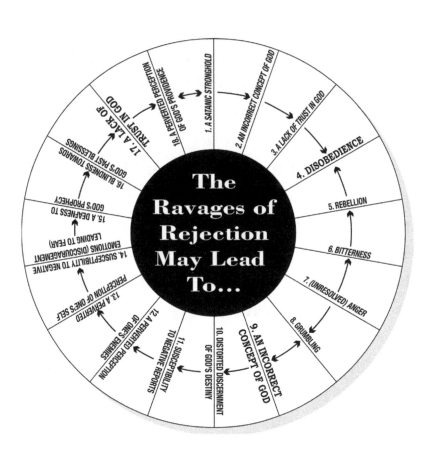

The
Ravages of
Rejection
May Lead
To...

1. A SATANIC STRONGHOLD
2. AN INCORRECT CONCEPT OF GOD
3. A LACK OF TRUST IN GOD
4. DISOBEDIENCE
5. REBELLION
6. BITTERNESS
7. (UNRESOLVED) ANGER
8. GRUMBLING
9. AN INCORRECT CONCEPT OF GOD
10. DISTORTED DISCERNMENT OF GOD'S DESTINY
11. A SUSCEPTIBILITY TO NEGATIVE REPORTS
12. A PERVERTED PERCEPTION OF ONE'S ENEMIES
13. A PERVERTED PERCEPTION OF ONE'S SELF
14. SUSCEPTIBILITY TO NEGATIVE EMOTIONS (DISCOURAGEMENT LEADING TO FEAR)
15. A DEAFNESS TO GOD'S PROPHECY
16. BLINDNESS TOWARDS GOD'S PAST BLESSINGS
17. A LACK OF TRUST IN GOD
18. A PERVERTED PERCEPTION OF GOD'S PROVIDENCE

CPSIA information can be obtained
at www.ICGtesting.com
Printed in the USA
LVHW050015270723
753307LV00013B/1214